NIST
National Institute of
Standards and Technology
U.S. Department of Commerce

Special Publication 800-147

BIOS Protection Guidelines

Recommendations of the National Institute of Standards and Technology

David Cooper
William Polk
Andrew Regenscheid
Murugiah Souppaya

NIST Special Publication 800-147

BIOS Protection Guidelines

Recommendations of the National Institute of Standards and Technology

David Cooper
William Polk
Andrew Regenscheid
Murugiah Souppaya

COMPUTER SECURITY

Computer Security Division
Information Technology Laboratory
National Institute of Standards and Technology
Gaithersburg, MD 20899-8930

April 2011

U.S. Department of Commerce

Gary Locke, Secretary

National Institute of Standards and Technology

Dr. Patrick D. Gallagher, Director

Reports on Computer Systems Technology

The Information Technology Laboratory (ITL) at the National Institute of Standards and Technology (NIST) promotes the U.S. economy and public welfare by providing technical leadership for the nation's measurement and standards infrastructure. ITL develops tests, test methods, reference data, proof of concept implementations, and technical analysis to advance the development and productive use of information technology. ITL's responsibilities include the development of technical, physical, administrative, and management standards and guidelines for the cost-effective security and privacy of sensitive unclassified information in Federal computer systems. This Special Publication 800-series reports on ITL's research, guidance, and outreach efforts in computer security and its collaborative activities with industry, government, and academic organizations.

National Institute of Standards and Technology Special Publication 800-147
Natl. Inst. Stand. Technol. Spec. Publ. 800-147, 27 pages (April 2011)

Acknowledgments

The authors, David Cooper, William Polk, Andrew Regenscheid, and Murugiah Souppaya of the National Institute of Standards and Technology (NIST) wish to thank their colleagues who reviewed drafts of this document and contributed to its technical content. The authors gratefully acknowledge and appreciate the contributions from individuals and organizations that submitted comments on the public draft of this publication. The comments and suggestions helped to improve the overall quality of the document.

In addition, the authors would also like to thank Gustavo Duarte, who created an earlier diagram of the boot-up process that was used as the basis for Figures 1 and 2 in this document.

Table of Contents

List of Appendices

Executive Summary

Modern computers rely on fundamental system firmware, commonly known as the system Basic Input/Output System (BIOS), to facilitate the hardware initialization process and transition control to the operating system. The BIOS is typically developed by both original equipment manufacturers (OEMs) and independent BIOS vendors, and is distributed to end-users by motherboard or computer manufacturers. Manufacturers frequently update system firmware to fix bugs, patch vulnerabilities, and support new hardware. This document provides security guidelines for preventing the unauthorized modification of BIOS firmware on PC client systems.

Unauthorized modification of BIOS firmware by malicious software constitutes a significant threat because of the BIOS's unique and privileged position within the PC architecture. A malicious BIOS modification could be part of a sophisticated, targeted attack on an organization—either a permanent denial of service (if the BIOS is corrupted) or a persistent malware presence (if the BIOS is implanted with malware). The move from conventional BIOS implementations to implementations based on the Unified Extensible Firmware Interface (UEFI) may make it easier for malware to target the BIOS in a widespread fashion, as these BIOS implementations are based on a common specification.

This document focuses on current and future x86 and x64 desktop and laptop systems, although the controls and procedures could potentially apply to any system design. Likewise, although the guide is oriented toward enterprise-class platforms, the necessary technologies are expected to migrate to consumer-grade systems over time. The security guidelines do not attempt to prevent installation of unauthentic BIOSs through the supply chain, by physical replacement of the BIOS chip, or through secure local update procedures.

Security guidelines are specified for four system BIOS features:
- The authenticated BIOS update mechanism, where digital signatures prevent the installation of BIOS update images that are not authentic.
- An optional secure local update mechanism, where physical presence authorizes installation of BIOS update images.
- Integrity protection features, to prevent unintended or malicious modification of the BIOS outside the authenticated BIOS update process.
- Non-bypassability features, to ensure that there are no mechanisms that allow the system processor or any other system component to bypass the authenticated update mechanism.

Additionally, management best practices which complement the security guidelines are presented. Five distinct phases are addressed:
- The Provisioning Phase, which establishes configuration baselines identifying the approved BIOS version and configuration settings.
- The Platform Deployment Phase, which establishes or verifies the configuration baseline using a secure local update mechanism.
- The Operations and Maintenance Phase, where systems are monitored for unexpected changes and planned BIOS updates are executed using the authenticated BIOS update mechanism.
- The Recovery Phase, which supports authorized rollback to an earlier BIOS version and recovery from a corrupted BIOS.
- The Disposition Phase, where the BIOS and configuration data are restored to their original settings to prevent against accidental information leakage.

Future revisions to this publication will also address the security of critical system firmware that interact with the BIOS.

1. Introduction

1.1 Authority

The National Institute of Standards and Technology (NIST) developed this document in furtherance of its statutory responsibilities under the Federal Information Security Management Act (FISMA) of 2002, Public Law 107-347.

NIST is responsible for developing standards and guidelines, including minimum requirements, for providing adequate information security for all agency operations and assets; but such standards and guidelines shall not apply to national security systems. This guideline is consistent with the requirements of the Office of Management and Budget (OMB) Circular A-130, Section 8b(3), "Securing Agency Information Systems," as analyzed in A-130, Appendix IV: Analysis of Key Sections. Supplemental information is provided in A-130, Appendix III.

This guideline has been prepared for use by Federal agencies. It may be used by nongovernmental organizations on a voluntary basis and is not subject to copyright, though attribution is desired.

Nothing in this document should be taken to contradict standards and guidelines made mandatory and binding on Federal agencies by the Secretary of Commerce under statutory authority, nor should these guidelines be interpreted as altering or superseding the existing authorities of the Secretary of Commerce, Director of the OMB, or any other Federal official.

1.2 Purpose and Scope

This document provides guidelines for preventing the unauthorized modification of *Basic Input/Output System (BIOS)* firmware on PC client systems. Unauthorized modification of BIOS firmware by malicious software constitutes a significant threat because of the BIOS's unique and privileged position within the PC architecture. A malicious BIOS modification could be part of a sophisticated, targeted attack on an organization —either a permanent denial of service (if the BIOS is corrupted) or a persistent malware presence (if the BIOS is implanted with malware).

As used in this publication, the term BIOS refers to conventional BIOS, *Extensible Firmware Interface (EFI)* BIOS, and *Unified Extensible Firmware Interface (UEFI)* BIOS. This document applies to system BIOS firmware (e.g., conventional BIOS or UEFI BIOS) stored in the system flash memory of computer systems, including portions that may be formatted as Option ROMs. However, it does not apply to Option ROMs, UEFI drivers, and firmware stored elsewhere in a computer system.

Section 3.1 of this guide provides platform vendors with recommendations and guidelines for a secure BIOS update process. Additionally, Section 3.2 provides recommendations for managing the BIOS in an operational environment. Future revisions to this publication will also address the security of critical system firmware that interact with the BIOS.

While this document focuses on current and future x86 and x64 client platforms, the controls and procedures are independent of any particular system design. Likewise, although the guide is oriented toward enterprise-class platforms, the necessary technologies are expected to migrate to consumer-grade systems over time. Future efforts may look at boot firmware security for enterprise server platforms.

1.3 Audience

The intended audience for this document includes BIOS and platform vendors, and information system security professionals who are responsible for managing the endpoint platforms' security, secure boot processes, and hardware security modules. The material may also be of use when developing enterprise-wide procurement strategies and deployment.

The material in this document is technically oriented, and it is assumed that readers have at least a basic understanding of system and network security. The document provides background information to help such readers understand the topics that are discussed. Readers are encouraged to take advantage of other resources (including those listed in this document) for more detailed information.

1.4 Document Structure

The remainder of this document is organized into the following major sections:

- Section 2 presents an overview of the BIOS and its role in the boot process, and identifies potential attacks against the BIOS in an operational environment.

- Section 3 examines how selected threats to the BIOS can be mitigated. Section 3.1 describes security controls for BIOS implementations that are required or recommended to mitigate these threats. Section 3.2 defines processes that leverage these controls to implement a secure BIOS update process within an enterprise as part of the platform management life cycle.

The document also contains appendices with supporting material:

- Appendix A contains a summary of the security guidelines for system BIOS implementations.

- Appendix B defines terms used in this document.

- Appendix C contains a list of acronyms and abbreviations used in this document.

- Appendix D contains a list of references used in the development of this document.

2. Background

Modern computers such as desktop and laptop computers contain program code that facilitates the hardware initialization process. The code is stored in non-volatile memory and is commonly referred to as boot firmware. The primary firmware used to initialize the system is called the *Basic Input/Output System (BIOS)* or the *system BIOS*. This section provides background information on the system BIOS and its role in the boot process using the conventional BIOS and Unified Extensible Firmware Interface (UEFI) BIOS as examples. It identifies the primary methods used for updating the system BIOS, and security issues and threats to the system BIOS.

2.1 System BIOS

The system BIOS is the first piece of software executed on the main central processing unit (CPU) when a computer is powered on. While the system BIOS was originally responsible for providing operating systems access to hardware, its primary role on modern machines is to initialize and test hardware components and load the operating system. In addition, the BIOS loads and initializes important system management functions, such as power and thermal management. The system BIOS may also load CPU microcode patches during the boot process.

There are several different types of BIOS firmware. Some computers use a16-bit conventional BIOS, while many newer systems use boot firmware based on the UEFI specifications [UEFI]. In this document we refer to all types of boot firmware as BIOS firmware, the system BIOS, or simply BIOS. When necessary, we differentiate conventional BIOS firmware from UEFI firmware by calling them the conventional BIOS and UEFI BIOS, respectively.

System BIOS is typically developed by both original equipment manufacturers (OEMs) and independent BIOS vendors, and is distributed to end users with computer hardware. Manufacturers frequently update system firmware to fix bugs, patch vulnerabilities, and support new hardware. The system BIOS is typically stored on electrically erasable programmable read-only memory (EEPROM) or other forms of flash memory, and is modifiable by end users. Typically, system BIOS firmware is updated using a utility or tool that has special knowledge of the non-volatile storage components in which the BIOS is stored.

A given computer system can have BIOS in several different locations. In addition to the motherboard, BIOS can be found on hard drive controllers, video cards, network cards and other add-in cards. This additional firmware generally takes the form of *Option ROMs* (containing conventional BIOS and/or UEFI drivers). These are loaded and executed by the system firmware during the boot process. Other system devices, such as hard drives and optical drives, may have their own microcontrollers and other types of firmware.

As noted in Section 1.2, the guidelines in this document apply BIOS firmware stored in the system flash. This includes Option ROMs and UEFI drivers that are stored with the system BIOS firmware and are updated by the same mechanism. It does not apply to Option ROMs, UEFI drivers, and firmware stored elsewhere in a computer system.

2.2 Role of System BIOS in the Boot Process

The primary function of the system BIOS is to initialize important hardware components and to load the operating system. This process is known as *booting*. The boot process of the system BIOS typically executes in the following stages:

1. **Execute Core Root of Trust:** The system BIOS may include a small core block of firmware that executes first and is capable of verifying the integrity of other firmware components. This has traditionally been called the *BIOS Boot Block*. For trusted computing applications, it may also contain the Core Root of Trust for Measurement (CRTM).
2. **Initialize and Test Low-Level Hardware:** Very early in the boot process the system BIOS initializes and tests key pieces of hardware on the computer system, including the motherboard, chipset, memory and CPU.
3. **Load and Execute Additional Firmware Modules:** The system BIOS executes additional pieces of firmware that either extend the capabilities of the system BIOS or initialize other hardware components necessary for booting the system. These additional modules may be stored within the same flash memory as the system BIOS or they may be stored in the hardware devices they initialize (e.g., video card, local area network card).
4. **Select Boot Device:** After system hardware has been configured, the system BIOS searches for a boot device (e.g., hard drive, optical drive, USB drive) and executes the boot loader stored on that device.
5. **Load Operating System**: While the system BIOS is still in control of the computer, the boot loader begins to load and initialize the operating system kernel. Once the kernel is functional, primary control of the computer system transfers from the system BIOS to the operating system.

In addition, the system BIOS loads system management interrupt (SMI) handlers (also known as System Management Mode (SMM) code) and initializes Advanced Configuration and Power Interface (ACPI) tables and code. These provide important system management functions for the running computer system, such as power and thermal management.

This section describes the boot process in conventional BIOS-based systems and the boot process in UEFI-based systems. While conventional BIOS is used in many desktop and laptop computers deployed today, the industry has begun transitioning to UEFI BIOS.

2.2.1 Conventional BIOS Boot Process

Figure 1 shows a typical boot process for x86-compatible systems running a conventional BIOS. The conventional BIOS often executes in 16-bit real mode, although some more recent implementations execute in protected mode. Some conventional BIOS-based firmware has a small block of BIOS firmware— known as the BIOS boot block— that is logically separate from the rest of the BIOS. On these computer systems, the boot block is the first firmware executed during the boot process. The boot block is responsible for checking the integrity of the remaining BIOS code, and may provide mechanisms for recovery if the main system BIOS firmware is corrupted. On most trusted computing architectures, the BIOS boot block serves as the computer system's CRTM because this firmware is implicitly trusted to bootstrap the process of building a measurement chain for subsequent attestation of other firmware and software that is executed on the machine [TCG05].

The boot block executes the part of the conventional BIOS that initializes most hardware components— the *Power-on-Self-Test* (POST) code. During POST, key low-level hardware on the computer system is initialized, including the chipset, CPU, and memory. The system BIOS initializes the video card, which may load and execute its own BIOS to initialize graphics processors and memory.

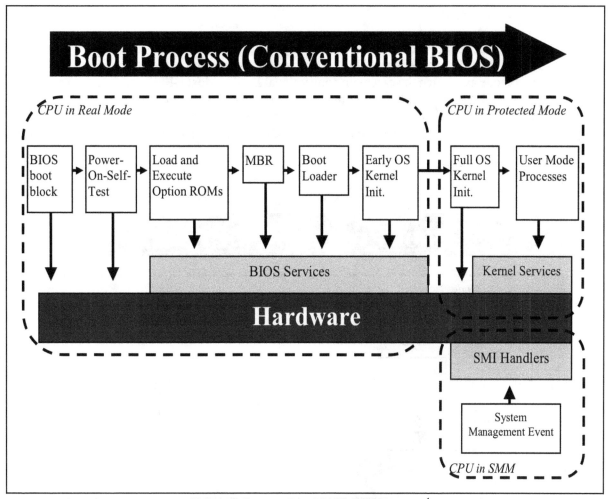

Figure 1: Conventional BIOS Boot Process[1]

Next, the system BIOS searches for other peripherals and microcontrollers, and executes any Option ROMs on these components necessary to initialize them. Option ROMs execute very early in the boot process and can add a variety of features to the boot process. For example, the Option ROM on a network adapter could load the Preboot Execution Environment (PXE), which allows a computer to boot over the network.

Next, the system BIOS scans the computer system for storage devices that have been identified as boot devices. In a typical case, the BIOS attempts to boot from the first boot device it finds that has a valid master boot record (MBR). The MBR points to a boot loader stored on the hard drive, which in turn starts the process of loading the operating system.

During the boot process the system BIOS loads SMI handlers and initializes ACPI tables and code. SMI handlers run in a special high-privilege mode on the CPU known as System Management Mode, a 32-bit mode that is capable of bypassing many of the hardware security mechanisms of protected mode, such as memory segmentation and page protections.

---

[1] This figure is based on information and a diagram found at [Duarte08].

2.2.2 UEFI Boot Process

At a high level, the UEFI boot process, shown in Figure 2, follows a similar flow to the conventional BIOS boot process. One difference is that UEFI code runs in 32- or 64-bit protected mode on the CPU, not in 16-bit real mode as is often the case with conventional BIOS. Most UEFI-based platforms start with a small core block of code that has the primary responsibility of authenticating subsequent code executed on the computer system. This is very similar to the role of the boot block in conventional BIOS. This part of the boot process is known as the Security (SEC) phase, and it serves as the core root of trust in the computer system.

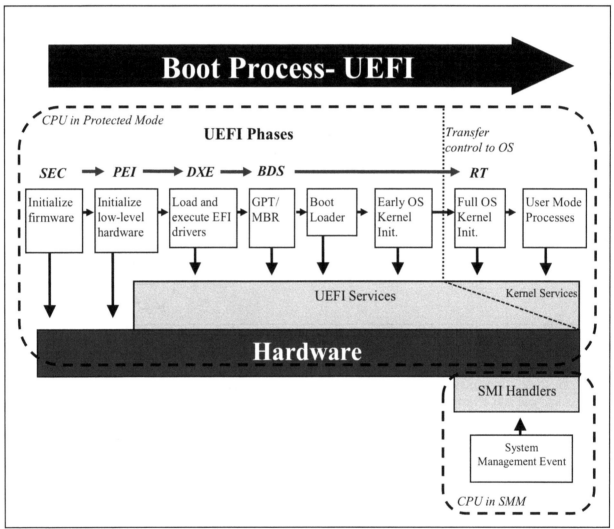

Figure 2: UEFI BIOS Boot Process

The next phase of the UEFI boot process is the Pre-EFI Initialization (PEI) Phase. The PEI phase is intended to initialize key system components, such as the processor, chipset and motherboard. In some cases, the code in the Security Phase and the PEI Phase comprise the core root of trust in a UEFI system.

The purpose of the PEI Phase is to prepare the system for the Driver Execution Environment (DXE) phase. The DXE phase is where most system initialization is performed. The firmware executed in this phase is responsible for searching for and executing drivers that provide device support during the boot process, or provide additional features. During this phase the UEFI BIOS may execute conventional option ROMs, which have a similar purpose.

The PEI and DXE phases of the UEFI boot process lay the foundation to load an operating system. The final tasks necessary to load an operating system are performed in the Boot Device Selection (BDS) phase. This phase initializes console devices for simple input/output operations on the system. These console devices include local text or graphical interfaces, as well as remote interfaces, such as Telnet or remote displays over HTTP. The BDS phase also loads any additional drivers necessary to manage console or boot devices. Finally, the firmware loads the boot loader from the first MBR or GUID Partition Table (GPT) formatted boot device, and loads the operating system.

During the boot process the UEFI BIOS loads SMI handlers and initializes ACPI tables and code.

The Run Time phase of the UEFI boot process begins when the operating system is ready to take control from the UEFI BIOS. UEFI runtime services are available to the operating system during this phase.

2.3   Updating the System BIOS

A system and its supporting management software and firmware may provide several authorized mechanisms for legitimately updating the system BIOS. These include:
1. **User-Initiated Updates:** System and motherboard manufacturers typically supply end users with utilities capable of updating the system BIOS. Historically, end users booted from external media to perform these updates, but today most manufacturers provide utilities that can update the system BIOS from the user's normal operating system. Depending on the security mechanisms implemented on the system, these utilities might directly update the system BIOS or they may schedule an update for the next system reboot.
2. **Managed Updates:** A given computer system may have hardware and software-based agents that allow a system administrator to remotely update the system BIOS without direct involvement from the user.
3. **Rollback:** System BIOS implementations that authenticate updates before applying them may also check version numbers during the update process. In these cases, the system BIOS may have a special update process for rolling back the installed firmware to an earlier version. For instance, the rollback process might require the physical presence of the user. This mechanism guards against attackers flashing old firmware with known vulnerabilities.
4. **Manual Recovery:** To recover from a corrupt or malfunctioning system BIOS, many computer systems provide mechanisms to allow a user with physical presence during the boot process to replace the current system BIOS with a known good version and configuration.
5. **Automatic Recovery:** Some computer systems are able to detect when the system BIOS has been corrupted and recover from a backup firmware image stored in a separate storage location from the primary system BIOS (e.g., a second flash memory chip, a hidden partition on a hard drive).

2.4   Importance of BIOS Integrity

As the first code that is executed by the main CPU, the system BIOS is a critical security component of a computer system. While the system BIOS, possibly with the use of a Trusted Platform Module (TPM), can verify the integrity of firmware and software executed later in the boot process, typically all or part of the system BIOS is implicitly trusted.

The system BIOS is a potentially attractive target for attack. Malicious code running at the BIOS level could have a great deal of control over a computer system. It could be used to compromise any components that are loaded later in the boot process, including the SMM code, boot loader, hypervisor, and operating system. The BIOS is stored on non-volatile memory that persists between power cycles. Malware written into a BIOS could be used to re-infect machines even after new operating systems have been installed or hard drives replaced. Because the system BIOS runs early in the boot process with very high privileges on the machine, malware running at the BIOS level may be very difficult to detect. Because the BIOS loads first, there is no opportunity for anti-malware products to authoritatively scan the BIOS.

BIOS exploits would likely be highly system-specific—directed at a specific version of a system BIOS or certain hardware components (e.g., a particular motherboard chipset). In contrast, most malware targets software executing at or above the operating system kernel, where it is easier to develop and can attack larger classes of machines. BIOS-level malware may be more likely employed in targeted attacks on high-value computer systems. The move to UEFI-based BIOS may make it easier for malware to target the BIOS in a widespread fashion, as these BIOS implementations are based on a common specification.

For the reasons outlined above, there are few known instances of BIOS-level malware. At this time, the only publicly known malware targeting the system BIOS that has infected a significant number of computers is the CIH virus, also known as the Chernobyl virus [Sym02], first discovered in 1998. One element of the payload of this virus attempted to overwrite the BIOS on systems using a specific chipset that was widely deployed at the time. This malware relied on several vulnerabilities that are not present in modern machines.

Security researchers have demonstrated other potential attacks on conventional BIOS and EFI/UEFI firmware. Proof-of-concept attacks have been demonstrated that allow for the insertion of malicious code into conventional BIOS implementations that permit unsigned updates [SaOr09]. Other researchers have discovered a buffer-overflow vulnerability in the EFI BIOS on a modern platform. Although this EFI BIOS write-protects firmware early in the boot process and only flashes signed updates to firmware, the buffer overflow allowed the researchers to bypass the secure update process by executing an unsigned portion of the firmware update package before write protections were applied [WoTe09].

Vulnerabilities such as these could allow attackers to create stealthy malware that operate with very high privileges on a system. The system BIOS loads SMI handlers before passing control of the computer to the operating system. Malicious code written into a BIOS could modify the SMI handlers to create malware that would run in SMM [EmSp08]. This would give the malware unrestricted access to physical memory and peripherals connected to the host machine, and it would be very difficult for software running on the operating system to detect.

2.5   Threats to the System BIOS

The preceding section established the importance of maintaining the integrity of the system BIOS. This section describes some of the various ways that the integrity of the system BIOS can be attacked, and identifies the attacks considered within scope for the security controls and processes specified in Section 3.

The first threat to the integrity of the system BIOS comes while the system moves through the supply chain. Supply chain security techniques are out of scope for the security controls specified in this document. Some of the procedures specified in Section 3.2 can, however, be used to identify and remedy systems that have an unapproved system BIOS.

Assuming that the system arrives with the manufacturer's intended system BIOS installed, there are a number of threats to the integrity of the system BIOS during the system's lifetime:

- One of the most difficult threats to prevent is a user-initiated installation of a malicious system BIOS. User-initiated BIOS update utilities are often the primary method for updating the system BIOS. The guidelines included in this document will not prevent users from installing unapproved BIOS images if they have physical access to the computer system. As with supply chain threats, security processes may be able to detect and remediate the unapproved system BIOS, such as initiating a recovery process to restore to an approved BIOS.

- Malware could leverage weak BIOS security controls or exploit vulnerabilities in the system BIOS itself to reflash or modify the system BIOS. General-purpose malicious software is unlikely to include this functionality, but a targeted attack on an organization could be directed towards an organization's standard system BIOS. The malicious BIOS can be delivered to the system either over a network, or using media. The guidelines presented in this document are designed to prevent these kinds of attack.

- Network-based system management tools could also be used to launch an organization-wide attack on system BIOSs. For example, consider an organization-maintained update server for the organization's deployed system BIOS; a compromised server could push a malicious system BIOS to computer systems across the organization. This is a high-impact attack, but requires either an insider or compromise of an organization's update process. The guidelines presented in this document are designed to prevent this kind of attack.

- Any of the preceding mechanisms could be used to rollback to an authentic but vulnerable system BIOS. This is a particularly insidious attack, since the "bad" BIOS is authentic (i.e., shipped by the manufacturer). The security controls specified in the following section are primarily focused on verifying the source and integrity of the system BIOS. This document includes recommended controls for rollback protection.

The controls described in the following section are primarily focused on preventing unauthorized modification of the system BIOS by potentially malicious software running on computer systems. Installation of an unapproved system BIOS in the supply chain, by individuals with physical access, or through rollback to an authenticated but vulnerable system BIOS, are not addressed by the controls in Section 3.1, but can be addressed using processes specified in Section 3.2.

3. Threat Mitigation

BIOS is a critical component of a secure system. As the first code executed during the boot process, the system BIOS is implicitly trusted by hardware and software components in a system. The previous section described the system BIOS's role in the boot process, the system BIOS's appeal to attackers, and the potential threats resulting in the unauthorized modification of the BIOS. This section presents security guidelines for BIOS implementations and recommended practices for managing BIOSs in an enterprise environment. Section 3.1 provides guidelines for a secure BIOS update process. It is intended for platform vendors designing, implementing, or selecting a system BIOS implementation. While products may not be immediately available, organizations can use these guidelines at input to their procurement processes and begin developing plans to make use of these security features when they are available. Organizations can use the recommended BIOS management practices in Section 3.2 when developing these plans. The recommendations are intended to prevent unauthorized modification of the BIOS.

3.1 Security Guidelines for System BIOS Implementations

This subsection provides guidelines intended to maintain the integrity of the BIOS after it has been provisioned by securing the mechanisms used for updating the BIOS. In particular, this subsection defines guidelines for system BIOS implementations for a secure BIOS update mechanism. A secure BIOS update mechanism includes:
1. a process for verifying the authenticity and integrity of BIOS updates; and
2. a mechanism for ensuring that the BIOS is protected from modification outside of the secure update process.

Authentication verifies that a BIOS update image was generated by an authentic source and is unaltered. All updates to the system BIOS shall either go through an authenticated BIOS update mechanism as described in Section 3.1.1 or use an optional secure local update mechanism compliant with the guidelines in Section 3.1.2.

These guidelines for a secure BIOS update mechanism do not mitigate all risks associated with the system BIOS. Some threats to unauthorized modification of the system BIOS remain. For example, these guidelines do not prevent individuals with physical access to systems from modifying the system BIOS. Nor do they guarantee the absence of vulnerabilities in the system BIOS implementations. The guidelines on the system BIOS should be used in conjunction with organizations' existing security policies and procedures.

3.1.1 BIOS Update Authentication

The authenticated BIOS update mechanism employs digital signatures to ensure the authenticity of the BIOS update image. To update the BIOS using the authenticated BIOS update mechanism, there shall be a Root of Trust for Update (RTU) that contains a signature verification algorithm and a key store that includes the public key needed to verify the signature on the BIOS update image. The key store and the signature verification algorithm shall be stored in a protected fashion on the computer system and shall be modifiable only using an authenticated update mechanism or a secure local update mechanism as outlined in Section 3.1.2.

The key store in the RTU shall include a public key used to verify the signature on a BIOS update image or include a hash [FIPS 180-3] of the public key if a copy of the public key is provided with the BIOS update image. In the latter case, the update mechanism shall hash the public key provided with the BIOS update image and ensure that it matches a hash which appears in the key store before using the provided public key to verify the signature on the BIOS update image.

BIOS images shall be signed in conformance with NIST SP 800-89, *Recommendation for Obtaining Assurances for Digital Signature Applications* [SP800-89], using an approved digital signature algorithm as specified in NIST FIPS 186-3, *Digital Signature Standard* [FIPS186-3], that provides at least 112 bits of security strength, in accordance with NIST SP 800-131A, *Transitions: Recommendation for Transitioning the Use of Cryptographic Algorithms and Key Lengths* [SP800-131A].

The update mechanism shall ensure that the BIOS update image has been digitally signed and that the digital signature can be verified using a key in the RTU before updating the BIOS. Recovery mechanisms shall also use the authenticated update mechanism unless the recovery process meets the guidelines for a secure local update. The authenticated update mechanism should prevent the unauthorized rollback of the BIOS to an earlier authentic version that has a known security weakness. This limitation of the rollback mechanism may be accomplished, for example, by verifying that the version number of the BIOS image is larger than the currently installed BIOS image's version number.

Some organizations may wish to assert greater control over BIOS updates in high-security environments. The authenticated update mechanism may be designed to permit organizational control over the update process, where updates to the BIOS or rollbacks of the BIOS to an earlier version are permitted only if the update or rollback has been authorized by the organization. For example, specific BIOS images could be authorized by an organization by countersigning them with an organization-controlled key, which would be verified during the update process.

3.1.2 Secure Local Update

BIOS implementations may optionally include a secure local update mechanism that updates the system BIOS without using the authenticated update mechanism. The secure local update mechanism, if it is implemented, should be used only to load the first BIOS image or to recover from a corruption of a system BIOS that cannot be fixed using the authenticated update mechanism described in Section 3.1.1. A secure local update mechanism shall ensure the authenticity and integrity of the BIOS update image by requiring physical presence. Further protections may be implemented in the secure local update mechanism by requiring the entry of an administrator password or the unlocking of a physical lock (e.g., a motherboard jumper) before permitting the system BIOS to be updated.

3.1.3 Integrity Protection

To prevent unintended or malicious modification of the system BIOS outside the authenticated BIOS update process, the RTU and the system BIOS (excluding configuration data used by the system BIOS that is stored in non-volatile memory) shall be protected from unintended or malicious modification with a mechanism that cannot be overridden outside of an authenticated BIOS update. The protection mechanism shall itself be protected from unauthorized modification.

The authenticated BIOS update mechanism shall be protected from unintended or malicious modification by a mechanism that is at least as strong as that protecting the RTU and the system BIOS.

The protection mechanism shall protect relevant regions of the system flash memory containing the system BIOS prior to executing firmware or software that can be modified without using an authenticated update mechanism or a secure local update mechanism. Protections should be enforced by hardware mechanisms that are not alterable except by an authorized mechanism.

3.1.4 Non-Bypassability

The authenticated BIOS update mechanism shall be the exclusive mechanism for modifying the system BIOS absent physical intervention through the secure local update mechanism. The design of the system and accompanying system components and firmware shall ensure that there are no mechanisms that allow the system processor or any other system component to bypass the authenticated update mechanism, except for the secure local update mechanism. Any such mechanisms capable of bypassing the authenticated update mechanism could create a vulnerability allowing malicious software to modify the system BIOS or overwrite the system flash with a BIOS image from an illegitimate source.

A modern platform includes design features that give system components direct access to the system BIOS for performance improvements, such as shadowing the BIOS in RAM or for system management mode operations. System components may have read access to BIOS flash memory, but they shall not be able to directly modify the system BIOS except through the authenticated update mechanism or by an authorized mechanism requiring physical intervention. For example, bus mastering that bypasses the main processor (e.g., Direct Memory Access to the system flash) shall not be capable of directly modifying the firmware. Also, microcontrollers on the system shall not be capable of directly modifying the firmware, unless the hardware and firmware components of the microcontroller are protected with equivalent mechanisms at the RTU. These non-bypassability guidelines do not apply to configuration data used by the system BIOS that is stored in non-volatile memory.

3.2 Recommended Practices for BIOS Management

This section introduces considerations for managing system BIOS in an enterprise operational environment leveraging the existing policy, process, and operations practices. It focuses on key activities revolving around provisioning, deploying, managing, and decommissioning the system BIOS as part of its overall platform life cycle. Activities performed in a recovery phase are also specified to handle exceptional conditions.

Provisioning Phase: It is crucial that the organization institute a mechanism for identifying, inventorying, and tracking the different computer systems across the enterprise throughout their life cycle. Identifying and monitoring the BIOS image characteristics such as manufacturer name, version, or time stamp allows the organization to perform update, rollback, and recovery. The organization should maintain a "golden master image" for each approved system BIOS, including superseded versions, in secure offline storage.

If the platform has a configurable Root of Trust for Update (RTU), the organization needs to maintain a copy of the key store and signature verification algorithm. If the RTU is integrated into the system BIOS then this guideline is satisfied by maintaining the golden BIOS image. If the RTU is not integrated into the system BIOS, the security afforded the RTU should be at least as strong as that for the golden BIOS image.

Most organizations will rely upon the manufacturer as the source for the authenticated BIOS. In this case, the organization does not maintain any private keys, and the RTU contains only public keys provided by the manufacturer. Where the organization prefers to participate actively in the BIOS authentication process by countersigning some or all approved system BIOS updates, the RTU may contain one or more public keys associated with the organization. In this case, the organization must securely maintain the corresponding private key so that the next BIOS update can be signed. Private keys should be maintained under multi-party control to protect against insider attacks. For organizational keys, the corresponding public keys must also be maintained securely (to ensure authentication of origin).

In addition, a common configuration baseline for each platform must be created to conform to the organization's policy. The baseline should ensure that the integrity protection and non-bypassability features are enabled (if they are configurable), and organization policies for password policy and device boot order are enforced. Finally, the BIOS image information and associated baseline of settings for each platform should be documented in the configuration management plan.[2]

Platform Deployment Phase: The secure local update process should be used to provision the approved BIOS for that platform from the golden master image, the corresponding RTU should be installed, and BIOS-related configuration parameters established before computer systems are deployed. This will help the organization maintain a consistent, known starting posture. The organization should periodically perform assessments to confirm that the organization's BIOS policies, processes, and procedures are being followed properly.

Specifically, the procedures must ensure that the appropriate system BIOS is installed, the RTU contains all required keys and no unauthorized keys, and the integrity protection and non-bypassability features are enabled if they are configurable.

Operation and Maintenance Phase: This phase includes the operations and maintenance activities that are important for maintaining BIOS security and reliability in the operational environment. System BIOS updates should be performed using a change management process and the new approved version should be documented in the configuration plan, noting the previous BIOS image has been superseded.

The BIOS image and configuration baseline should be continuously monitored. If an unapproved deviation from this baseline is detected, the event should be investigated, documented, and remediated as part of incident response activities. The incident response plan should document the process and set of authorized tools that can be used to capture the evidence to help determine the root cause.[3] The secure local update mechanism should be used to recover from a BIOS image compromise.

When a new BIOS image is required to extend system capabilities, improve system reliability, or remediate software vulnerabilities, BIOS updates should be performed using the authenticated update process. Where the organization participates actively in the update process, the multi-party control process must be executed to retrieve the private key from secure storage and generate the digital signature. The BIOS installation package should also be signed, and the digital signature should be verified before execution. Once the update has executed successfully, the configuration baseline should be validated to confirm that the computer system is still in compliance with the organization's defined policy.

Recovery Phase: In some circumstances, a BIOS update will be required that cannot be accomplished using the authenticated update process. For example, a corrupted system BIOS or RTU may be unable to execute or invoke the authentication procedures. In this case, the appropriate system BIOS and/or RTU may be able to be installed using the secure local update process. In other cases, a BIOS update may have unintended consequences, forcing the organization to roll back to an earlier version. Extra steps may be required for an authenticated update to authorize rollback (if versioning or timestamps are compared during the standard authentication process), or the secure local update process may be required to reestablish a secure baseline. As with the Operations and Maintenance phase, it is essential to validate

---

[2] See Draft NIST SP 800-128, *Guide for Security Configuration Management of Information Systems* [SP800-128] for guidelines on developing a configuration management plan.
[3] For additional information on establishing incident response capabilities and handling incidents efficiently and effectively, see NIST SP 800-61rev1 *Computer Security Incident Handling Guide* [SP800-61].

the configuration of the BIOS against the organization's defined policy after BIOS rollback or reinstallation.

Disposition Phase: Before the computer system is disposed and leaves the organization, the organization should remove or destroy any sensitive data from the system BIOS. The configuration baseline should be reset to the manufacturer's default profile; in particular, sensitive settings such as passwords should be deleted from the system and keys should also be removed from the key store. If the system BIOS includes any organization-specific customizations then a vendor-provided BIOS image should be installed. This phase of the platform life cycle reduces chances for accidental data leakage.

Appendix A   Summary of Guidelines for System BIOS Implementations

This appendix contains a summary of the secure BIOS update guidelines for system BIOS implementations found in Section 3.1. These guidelines are intended for platform vendors designing, implementing, or selecting a system BIOS implementation. Readers should consult the relevant sections in the main body of this document for additional informative text that further describes the intent and context of the guidelines.

1. Approved BIOS Update Mechanisms

1-A   All updates to the system BIOS shall use either an authenticated BIOS update mechanism as described in Section 3.1.1 or an optional secure local update mechanism compliant with the guidelines in Section 3.1.2.

2. BIOS Update Authentication

2-A   There shall be a Root of Trust for Update (RTU) that contains a signature verification algorithm and a key store that includes the public key needed to verify the signature on the BIOS update image.

2-B   The key store and the signature verification algorithm shall be stored in a protected fashion on the computer system and shall be modifiable only using an authenticated update mechanism or a secure local update mechanism as outlined in Section 3.1.2.

2-C   The key store in the RTU shall include the public key for verifying the signature on a BIOS update image or include the hash [FIPS 180-3] of the public key for verifying the signature on a BIOS update image that includes the public key. In the latter case, the update mechanism shall ensure that the hash of the public key provided with the BIOS update image appears in the key store before using the provided public key to verify the signature on the BIOS update image.

2-D   BIOS images shall be signed in conformance with NIST SP 800-89, *Recommendation for Obtaining Assurances for Digital Signature Applications* [SP800-89], using an approved digital signature algorithm as specified in NIST FIPS 186-3, *Digital Signature Standard* [FIPS186-3], that provides at least 112 bits of security strength, in accordance with NIST SP 800-131A, *Transitions: Recommendation for Transitioning the Use of Cryptographic Algorithms and Key Lengths* [SP800-131A].

2-E   The authenticated update mechanism shall ensure that the BIOS update image has been digitally signed and that the digital signature can be verified using one of the keys in the key store in the RTU before updating the BIOS.

3. Secure Local Update (Optional)

BIOS implementations may optionally include a secure local update mechanism, where physical presence authorizes installation of BIOS update images without necessarily using the authenticate update mechanism.

3-A   A secure local update mechanism shall ensure the authenticity and integrity of the BIOS update image by requiring physical presence.

4. Integrity Protection

4-A The RTU and the BIOS (excluding configuration data used by the BIOS that is stored in non-volatile memory) shall be protected from unintended or malicious modification using a mechanism that cannot be overridden outside of an authenticated BIOS update.

4-B The protection mechanism shall be protected from unauthorized modification.

4-C The authenticated BIOS update mechanism shall be protected from unintended or malicious modification by a mechanism that is at least as strong as that protecting the RTU and the system BIOS.

4-D The protection mechanism shall protect relevant regions of the system flash memory containing the system BIOS prior to executing firmware or software that can be modified without using an authenticated update mechanism or a secure local update mechanism.

4-E Protections should be enforced by hardware mechanisms that are not alterable except by an authorized mechanism.

5. Non-Bypassability

These non-bypassability guidelines do not apply to configuration data used by the system BIOS that is stored in non-volatile memory.

5-A The authenticated BIOS update mechanism shall be the exclusive mechanism for modifying the system BIOS absent physical intervention through the secure local update mechanism.

5-B The design of the system and accompanying system components and firmware shall ensure that there are no mechanisms that allow the system processor or any other system component to bypass the authenticated update mechanism, except for the secure local update mechanism.

5-C While system components may have read access to BIOS flash memory, they shall not be able to directly modify the system BIOS except through the authenticated update mechanism or by an authorized mechanism requiring physical intervention.

5-C.i Bus mastering that bypasses the main processor (e.g., Direct Memory Access to the system flash) shall not be capable of directly modifying the firmware.

Microcontrollers on the system shall not be capable of directly modifying the firmware, unless the hardware and firmware components of the microcontroller are protected with equivalent mechanisms at the RTU.

Appendix B   Glossary

Selected terms used in the publication are defined below.

Basic Input/Output System (BIOS): In this publication, refers collectively to boot firmware based on the conventional BIOS, Extensible Firmware Interface (EFI), and the Unified Extensible Firmware Interface (UEFI).

Conventional BIOS: Legacy boot firmware used in many x86-compatible computer systems. Also known as the legacy BIOS.

Core Root of Trust for Measurement (CRTM): The first piece of BIOS code that executes on the main processor during the boot process. On a system with a Trusted Platform Module the CRTM is implicitly trusted to bootstrap the process of building a measurement chain for subsequent attestation of other firmware and software that is executed on the computer system.

Extensible Firmware Interface (EFI): A specification for the interface between the operating system and the platform firmware. Version 1.10 of the EFI specifications was the final version of the EFI specifications, and subsequent revisions made by the Unified EFI Forum are part of the UEFI specifications.

Firmware: Software that is included in read-only memory (ROM).

Option ROM: Firmware that is called by the system BIOS. Option ROMs include BIOS firmware on add-on cards (e.g., video card, hard drive controller, network card) as well as modules which extend the capabilities of the system BIOS.

Protected Mode: An operational mode found in x86-compatible processors with hardware support for memory protection, virtual memory, and multitasking.

Real Mode: A legacy high-privilege operating mode in x86-compatible processors.

System Management Mode (SMM): A high-privilege operating mode found in x86-compatible processors used for low-level system management functions. System Management Mode is only entered after the system generates a System Management Interrupt and only executes code from a segregated block of memory.

System Flash Memory: The non-volatile storage location of system BIOS, typically in electronically erasable programmable read-only memory (EEPROM) flash memory on the motherboard. While system flash memory is a technology-specific term, guidelines in this document referring to the system flash memory are intended to apply to any non-volatile storage medium containing the system BIOS.

Trusted Platform Module (TPM): A tamper-resistant integrated circuit built into some computer motherboards that can perform cryptographic operations (including key generation) and protect small amounts of sensitive information, such as passwords and cryptographic keys.

Unified Extensible Firmware Interface (UEFI): A possible replacement for the conventional BIOS that is becoming widely deployed in new x86-based computer systems. The UEFI specifications were preceded by the EFI specifications.

Appendix C   Acronyms and Abbreviations

This appendix contains a list of selected acronyms and abbreviations used in the guide.

ACPI	Advanced Configuration and Power Interface
BDS	Boot Device Selection
BIOS	Basic Input/Output System
CPU	Central Processing Unit
CRTM	Core Root of Trust for Measurement
DXE	Driver Execution Environment
EEPROM	Electrically Erasable Programmable Read-Only Memory
EFI	Extensible Firmware Interface
FIPS	Federal Information Processing Standard
FISMA	Federal Information Security Management Act
GPT	GUID Partition Table
GUID	Globally Unique Identifier
HTTP	Hypertext Transfer Protocol
IT	Information Technology
ITL	Information Technology Laboratory
MBR	Master Boot Record
NIST	National Institute of Standards and Technology
OEM	Original Equipment Manufacturer
OMB	Office of Management and Budget
OS	Operating System
PEI	Pre-EFI Initialization
POST	Power-on self-test
PXE	Preboot Execution Environment
ROM	Read-only Memory
RT	Runtime
RTU	Root of Trust for Update
SMI	System Management Interrupt
SMM	System Management Mode
SP	Special Publication
TPM	Trusted Platform Module
UEFI	Unified Extensible Firmware Interface

Appendix D   References

The list below provides references for this publication.

[Duarte08]   G. Duarte. "How Computers Boot Up." 5 June 2008.
http://www.duartes.org/gustavo/blog/post/how-computers-boot-up

[EFI]   *EFI 1.10 Specification.* Intel. 1 November 2003. http://www.intel.com/technology/efi/

[EmSp08]   Shawn Embleton, Sherri Sparks, and Cliff C. Zou. "SMM Rootkits: A New Breed of OS Independent Malware," *Proceedings of 4th International Conference on Security and Privacy in Communication Networks (SecureComm)*, Istanbul, Turkey, September 22-25, 2008.

[FIPS180-3]   FIPS 180-3, *Secure Hash Standard.* October 2008.

[FIPS186-3]   FIPS 186-3, *Digital Signature Standard.* June 2009.

[DuGr09]   Loïc Duflot, Olivier Grumelard, Olivier Levillain and Benjamin Morin. "ACPI and SMI handlers: some limits to trusted computing." *Journal in Computer Virology.* Volume 6, Number 4, 353-374.

[Graw09]   D. Grawrock. *Dynamics of a Trusted Platform: A Building Block Approach.* Hillsboro, OR: Intel Press, 2009.

[Heas07a]   J. Heasman. "Firmware Rootkits: A Threat to the Enterprise." Black Hat DC. Washington, DC. 28 February 2007.
http://www.nccgroup.com/Libraries/Document_Downloads/02_07_Firmware_Rootkits_The_Threat_to_the_Enterprise_Black_Hat_Washington_2007_sflb.sflb.ashx

[Heas07b]   J. Heasman. "Hacking the Extensible Firmware Interface." *Black Hat USA.* Las Vegas, NV. 2 August 2007. https://www.blackhat.com/presentations/bh-usa-07/Heasman/Presentation/bh-usa-07-heasman.pdf

[Intel03]   *Intel Platform Innovation Framework for EFI- Architecture Specification v0.9.* Intel. September 2003. http://www.intel.com/technology/framework/

[KGH09]   A. Kumar, G. Purushottam, and Y. Saint-Hilaire. *Active Platform Management Demystified.* Hillsboro, OR: Intel Press, 2009.

[Sal07]   Salihun, Darmawan. *BIOS Disassembly Ninjutsu Uncovered.* Wayne, PA: A-LIST, 2007.

[SaOr09]   A. Sacco, A. Ortéga. "Persistant BIOS Infection." *Phrack.* Issue 66. 6 November 2009. http://www.phrack.com/issues.html?issue=66&id=7

[SP800-57]   NIST SP 800-57, *Recommendation for Key Management – Part 1: General.* March 2007.

[SP800-61]   NIST SP 800-61rev1, *Computer Security Incident Handling Guide.* March 2008.

[SP800-89]   NIST SP 800-89, *Recommendation for Obtaining Assurances for Digital Signature Applications.* November 2006.

[SP800-128] Draft NIST SP 800-128, *Guide for Security Configuration Management of Information Systems.* March 2010.

[SP800-131A] NIST SP 800-131A, *Transitions: Recommendation for Transitioning the Use of Cryptographic Algorithms and Key Lengths.* January 2011.

[Sym02] *W95.CIH Technical Details*. Symantec. 25 April 2002.
http://www.symantec.com/security_response/writeup.jsp?docid=2000-122010-2655-99

[TCG05] *PC Client Work Group Specific Implementation Specification for Conventional Bios Specification, Version 1.2.* Trusted Computing Group. July 2005.
http://www.trustedcomputinggroup.org/resources/pc_client_work_group_specific_imple mentation_specification_for_conventional_bios_specification_version_12

[UEFI] *UEFI Specification Version 2.3.* Unified EFI Forum. May 2009.
http://www.uefi.org/specs/

[Wech09] F. Wecherowski. "A Real SMM Rootkit: Reversing and Hooking BIOS SMI Handlers." *Phrack.* Issue 66. 6 November 2009.
http://www.phrack.com/issues.html?issue=66&id=11

[WoTe09] R. Wojtczuk and A. Tereshkin. "Attacking Intel BIOS." *Black Hat USA*. Las Vegas, NV. 30 July 2009. http://www.blackhat.com/presentations/bh-usa-09/WOJTCZUK/BHUSA09-Wojtczuk-AtkIntelBios-SLIDES.pdf

National Institute of
Standards and Technology

U.S. Department of Commerce

Special Publication 800-155

(Draft)

BIOS Integrity Measurement Guidelines (Draft)

Recommendations of the National Institute of Standards and Technology

Andrew Regenscheid

Karen Scarfone

NIST Special Publication 800-155
(Draft)

BIOS Integrity Measurement Guidelines (Draft)

Recommendations of the National Institute of Standards and Technology

Andrew Regenscheid
Karen Scarfone

C O M P U T E R   S E C U R I T Y

Computer Security Division
Information Technology Laboratory
National Institute of Standards and Technology
Gaithersburg, MD 20899-8930

December 2011

U.S. Department of Commerce

John Bryson, Secretary

National Institute of Standards and Technology

Patrick D. Gallagher,
Under Secretary for Standards and Technology
and Director

Reports on Computer Systems Technology

The Information Technology Laboratory (ITL) at the National Institute of Standards and Technology (NIST) promotes the U.S. economy and public welfare by providing technical leadership for the nation's measurement and standards infrastructure. ITL develops tests, test methods, reference data, proof of concept implementations, and technical analysis to advance the development and productive use of information technology. ITL's responsibilities include the development of technical, physical, administrative, and management standards and guidelines for the cost-effective security and privacy of sensitive unclassified information in Federal computer systems. This Special Publication 800-series reports on ITL's research, guidance, and outreach efforts in computer security and its collaborative activities with industry, government, and academic organizations.

National Institute of Standards and Technology Special Publication 800-155 (Draft)
47 pages (Dec. 2011)

Acknowledgments

The authors wish to thank their colleagues who reviewed drafts of this document and contributed to its technical content. In particular, the authors would like to acknowledge the contributions of Greg Kazmierczak and Robert Thibadeau of Wave Systems, and Kurt Roemer from Citrix, who provided helpful comments and feedback on early drafts of this document. We would also like to thank our colleagues at NIST that reviewed early drafts of this document, including Bill Burr, Donna Dodson, Tim Polk, Matthew Scholl, Murugiah Souppaya, Bill Burr, and David Waltermire.

Abstract

This document outlines the security components and security guidelines needed to establish a secure Basic Input/Output System (BIOS) integrity measurement and reporting chain. Unauthorized modification of BIOS firmware constitutes a significant threat because of the BIOS's unique and privileged position within the PC architecture. The document focuses on two scenarios: detecting changes to the system BIOS code stored on the system flash, and detecting changes to the system BIOS configuration. The document is intended for hardware and software vendors that develop products that can support secure BIOS integrity measurement mechanisms, and may also be of use for organizations developing enterprise procurement or deployment strategies for these technologies.

Trademark Information

Table of Contents

List of Appendices

List of Figures

Executive Summary

Client computers such as desktops and laptops rely on the Basic Input/Output System (BIOS) to initialize their hardware during boot. The BIOS is firmware, and it can be configured. If the BIOS code or configuration is altered from the intended state, either maliciously or accidentally, the desktop or laptop may experience losses of confidentiality, integrity, and availability, including system instability, system failure, and information leakage. Also, the desktop or laptop could be vulnerable to more elaborate attacks such as covert monitoring, and it could be used as a stepping stone for attacking other systems. These consequences underscore why it is so important to detect changes to the BIOS code and configuration— and this can be accomplished by measuring and monitoring the integrity of the BIOS.

This publication explains the fundamentals of BIOS integrity measurement, such as basic requirements that must be met in order to measure BIOS integrity, and typical data flows for BIOS integrity measurement and reporting. This material provides a foundation for the core of the document, which presents guidelines to hardware and software vendors that develop products that can support secure BIOS integrity measurement mechanisms. These guidelines define in detail the requirements and recommendations for vendors to follow in support of BIOS integrity measurement.

The following are key requirements and recommendations for vendors supporting BIOS integrity measurement. Note that the formal declarations of these requirements and recommendations occur in Section 3; these are summaries and do not take the place of the more detailed Section 3 statements.

Provide the hardware support necessary to implement credible Roots of Trust for BIOS integrity measurements.

Roots of Trust are components (software, hardware, or hybrid) and computing engines that constitute a set of unconditionally trusted functions. Reliable and trustworthy BIOS integrity measurement and reporting depend upon software agents; each software agent relies upon Roots of Trust, and the level of trustworthiness in each agent depends on its Roots of Trust. BIOS integrity measurement requires the coordination of a Measurement Agent to harvest measurements, a Storage Agent to protect the measurements from modification until they can be reported, and a Reporting Agent to reliably report the measurements. Each of these agents has a corresponding Root of Trust (Root of Trust for Measurement, etc.) These Roots of Trust must act in concert and build on each other to enable reliable and trustworthy measurement, reporting, and verification of BIOS integrity measurements.

Enable endpoints to measure the integrity of all BIOS executable components and configuration data components at boot time.

A key factor in a meaningful integrity measurement comparison scheme is establishing and maintaining, with confidence, a known baseline of attributes and measurements. Endpoint vendors have various ways to convey attributes to users; regardless of how this is done, the reason for the attributes is to give the user a means of assessing the validity of the BIOS integrity measurements reported by the endpoint and developing a level of confidence in the reports it receives about the overall health status of the endpoint. This publication defines the attributes that endpoint vendors must provide and the minimal essential BIOS integrity measurements that all endpoints must be capable of reporting.

Securely transmit measurements of BIOS integrity from endpoints to the Measurement Assessment Authority (MAA).

When measurements are reliably and robustly reported, the MAA can accurately determine the state of the security relevant BIOS configuration items on each endpoint. This allows the MAA to report on and act upon the items with which the organization is concerned. Secure transmission of BIOS integrity measurements ensures that measurements are not modified, disclosed, or forged in transit by malicious parties. Further, proper selection of transmission protocols should ensure maximum interoperability, freshness, and efficiency.

1. Introduction

1.1 Authority

The National Institute of Standards and Technology (NIST) developed this document in furtherance of its statutory responsibilities under the Federal Information Security Management Act (FISMA) of 2002, Public Law 107-347.

NIST is responsible for developing standards and guidelines, including minimum requirements, for providing adequate information security for all agency operations and assets; however, such standards and guidelines shall not apply to national security systems. This guideline is consistent with the requirements of the Office of Management and Budget (OMB) Circular A-130, Section 8b (3), "Securing Agency Information Systems," as analyzed in A-130, Appendix IV: Analysis of Key Sections. Supplemental information is provided in A-130, Appendix III.

This guideline has been prepared for use by Federal agencies. It may be used by nongovernmental organizations on a voluntary basis and is not subject to copyright, although attribution is requested.

Nothing in this document should be taken to contradict standards and guidelines made mandatory and binding on Federal agencies by the Secretary of Commerce under statutory authority nor should these guidelines be interpreted as altering or superseding the existing authorities of the Secretary of Commerce, Director of the OMB, or any other Federal official.

1.2 Purpose and Scope

This document outlines the security components and security guidelines needed to establish a secure Basic Input/Output System (BIOS) integrity measurement and reporting chain. BIOS is a critical security component in systems due to its unique and privileged position within the personal computer (PC) architecture. A malicious or outdated BIOS could allow or be part of a sophisticated, targeted attack on an organization —either a permanent denial of service (if the BIOS is corrupted) or a persistent malware presence (if the BIOS is implanted with malware).

This document identifies two motivating scenarios in Section 2.1 for the guidelines in this document. First, the BIOS integrity measurement mechanisms are intended to detect changes to the system BIOS code stored on the system flash. Unauthorized changes to the system BIOS code could allow malicious software to run during the boot process. Second, the mechanisms are intended to detect changes to the configuration of the system BIOS. Unauthorized system BIOS configuration changes could place systems in insecure configurations, leaving them vulnerable to attack.

The guidelines in this document are intended to facilitate the development of products that can detect problems with the BIOS so that organizations can take appropriate remedial action to prevent or limit harm. The security controls and procedures specified in this document are oriented to desktops and laptops deployed in an enterprise environment.

While this publication focuses on security properties and capabilities for BIOS integrity measurement products, it will also provide administrators and security officers in organizations with a better understanding of the assurances that these types of products can provide, and the procedures that will need to be integrated into system previsioning and management processes once these technologies are deployed. The guidelines in this document can only be met with a combination of hardware and software support on devices spread across an organizations information technology infrastructure. This includes supporting roots of trust and security software on endpoint devices for obtaining and reporting measurements, support for requesting and interpreting measurements on enterprise-management systems, and potentially support on network devices to remediate problems. These components will be critical elements of a BIOS integrity measurement system.

1.3 Audience

The intended audience for this document includes hardware and software vendors that develop products that can support secure BIOS integrity measurement mechanisms. These include the endpoint vendor, typically the Original Equipment Manufacturer (OEM), the operating system (OS) vendor, and security application software vendors. System administrators and information system security professionals may also consult this document to understand the capabilities of these products and the procedures that will need to be incorporated into their system management processes when deploying these technologies.

The material in this document is technically oriented, and it is assumed that readers have at least a basic understanding of system and network security. The document provides background information to help such readers understand the topics that are discussed. Readers are encouraged to take advantage of other resources (including those listed in this document) for more detailed information.

1.4 Document Structure

The remainder of this document is organized into the following major sections and appendices:

- Section 2 presents an overview of BIOS integrity measurement and its role in the enterprise in detecting attacks against the BIOS in an operational environment.

- Section 3 describes the components necessary to measure the integrity of a BIOS and the security guidelines recommended for each component.

- Appendix A contains a summary of the security guidelines for system BIOS integrity measurement implementations.

- Appendix B defines acronyms, abbreviations, and terms used in this document.

- Appendix C identifies references.

- Appendix D contains a list of examples for how a company might choose to implement Roots of Trust.

- Appendix E contains a list of examples for how a company might choose to implement the guidelines using existing capabilities.

1.5 Document Conventions

The key words "MUST", "MUST NOT", "REQUIRED", "SHALL", "SHALL NOT", "SHOULD", "SHOULD NOT", "RECOMMENDED", "MAY", and "OPTIONAL" in this document are to be interpreted as described in Request for Comment (RFC) 2119 [IETF-RFC-2119]. When these words appear in regular case, such as "should" or "may", they are not intended to be interpreted as RFC 2119 key words.

Within this publication, the criteria for assigning requirements to MUST/SHALL, SHOULD, and MAY are as follows:

MUSTs/SHALLs: Requirements that are needed to support the scenarios outlined in Section 2, AND are feasible in the near term with currently available technology.

SHOULDs: Capabilities that are highly desirable and may be required in some circumstances to support a particular operational need or robustness level.

MAYs: Optional requirements that may be desirable under some circumstances.

2.   Background

Client computers such as desktops and laptops contain program code that facilitates the hardware initialization process. The code is stored in non-volatile memory and is commonly referred to as *boot firmware*. The primary firmware used to initialize the system is called the *Basic Input/Output System (BIOS)* or the *system BIOS*. If a BIOS is altered from its intended state, either maliciously or accidentally, the device on which it was altered may have a negative impact on the organization because the device is not necessarily operating in its intended state. Possible consequences include system instability, system failure, information leakage, and other losses of confidentiality, integrity, and availability. In addition, the system could be vulnerable to more elaborate attacks such as covert monitoring, and attackers could use the system as a stepping stone for attacking other systems. These examples illustrate why it is so important to detect changes to the BIOS and its configuration by measuring and monitoring its integrity.

This section provides an overview of BIOS integrity measurement (BIM) and its role in the organization in detecting, reporting, and mitigating attacks against the BIOS in an operational environment. The primary components required to accomplish this are identified and the threats addressed by this methodology are described.

2.1   BIOS Integrity Measurement Scenarios

This section presents scenarios that define candidate use cases, which drive the requirements and recommendations presented throughout the rest of this document. These use cases serve as a basis to identify user actions, associated transactions, inherent risks, and potential security mitigations.

The scenarios are predicated on objective state and process maturity for IT organizations in the area of BIM. To a large degree, this objective state closely mirrors the best practices employed by many organizations in the area of patch management for endpoints today. Specifically, organizations are expected to implement a provisioning process for new endpoints whereby BIM is fully integrated into the model. For example, provisioning an endpoint would include these additional BIOS integrity-specific activities that complement existing imaging, asset tracking, and registration activities:

- Installing and/or verifying the correct BIOS revision for a given client
- Imaging the BIOS with the appropriate BIOS settings
- Setting BIOS passwords
- Asserting any security controls requiring physical presence (which may include the Trusted Platform Module (TPM))
- Registering the endpoint identity and integrity metrics in the pertinent IT databases

Changes in any of these security variables may imply an anomalous situation and potentially more hazardous effects. Client operating system agents exist today that report basic information about these settings at the network management level, and they are a good initial tool for assessing BIOS security posture. As soon as feasible, though, these reporting agents need to be migrated to rely on integrity infrastructure anchored to tamperproof roots of trust.

2.1.1   Scenario 1: Something has changed in the system BIOS

BIOS updates are frequently released for client computers. These updates often fix bugs in the power management subsystem, hard disk or network management, or other important components. However, a BIOS could also be changed for malicious purposes. It is important that system administrators be able to

5

tell what version of BIOS is loaded on a device so as to be able to correctly manage it. This must be done while meeting the following basic challenges:

- IT management has to be able to trust that the measurements of BIOS firmware collected are correct.

  - There needs to be a root of trust to trust the collection of BIOS firmware integrity measurements.

  - An initial valid baseline of BIOS firmware integrity measurements must be collected, potentially using the device's root of trust to collect and report the baseline measurements.

  - BIOS firmware integrity measurements must be provably fresh (the response is not just a replay of an earlier good response).

  - BIOS firmware integrity measurements must have provable integrity (it has not changed between the responder and recipient).

  - The origin of BIOS firmware integrity measurements must be established (it came from the machine that IT thinks it came from).

- IT management has to be able to interpret reported BIOS firmware integrity measurements.

  - Standard formats are important.

  - The variability of systems needs to be accounted for.

- The users and administrators must know when something has changed in the BIOS without having to perform extensive calculations by hand.

2.1.2   Scenario 2: Something has changed in the BIOS configuration settings

BIOS settings have a large influence on the security of a system. A partial list of questions to be answered regarding settings includes:

- Passwords

  - Has the administrator password been set?

  - Has the Power On Password been set?

  - Has a hard disk password been set?

- BIOS-based management (BBM) software

  - Has it been turned on?

  - What is the configuration of the BIOS-based management software?

- Boot

  - Has the boot order changed?

  - Will the computer boot from anything other than the hard disk?

- Ports and other hardware interfaces

  - Are USB ports turned on?

  - Are 1394 ports turned on?

  - Are PCMCIA or smart card readers turned on?

o   Are Near Field Communication (NFC) ports turned on?

Any changes to these settings can indicate that the system has become less secure or has been compromised. Like the first scenario, it is important that both users and administrators be able to determine what the BIOS settings are and if they are within policy. This document requires capabilities that will allow the administrator to tell if a BIOS configuration setting has changed, and encourages the use of capabilities that will allow that administrator to distinguish which settings have changed.

BIOS configuration changes require the following, which are similar to, but extend the capabilities of BIOS code changes:

- IT management has to be able to trust that the BIOS configuration integrity measurements are correct.
  - o   There needs to be a root of trust to trust the BIOS configuration integrity measurements.
  - o   The measurements must be provably fresh.
  - o   The measurements must have provable integrity.
  - o   The origin of the measurements must be established.
- IT management has to be able to interpret the response.
  - o   Standard formats are important.
  - o   The variability of systems needs to be accounted for.

2.2   BIOS Integrity Measurement Flow

In order to measure BIOS integrity, certain basic requirements must be met, including:

- A means of generating and collecting the measurements
- A means of storing the measurements that is either tamper resistant or tamper evident
- A means of conveying the measurements to an analyzing agent
- A means of analyzing the measured result, and a means of administering a machine based on the results of that determination

The endpoint device must have a means of measuring the BIOS firmware and forwarding those measurements to an administrative authority. The endpoint must do this while protecting the integrity, authenticity, non-repudiation, and, in some cases, the confidentiality of those measurements.

Figure 1 illustrates the architecture that supports the generation, forwarding, and analysis of BIMs as well as remediation actions based on the analysis. These solutions may be provided by a single vendor or a combination of vendors. On the endpoint, the Roots of Trust for Measurement, Storage, and Reporting form the foundation for providing the necessary security services. Section 3.1 covers roots of trust in greater depth.

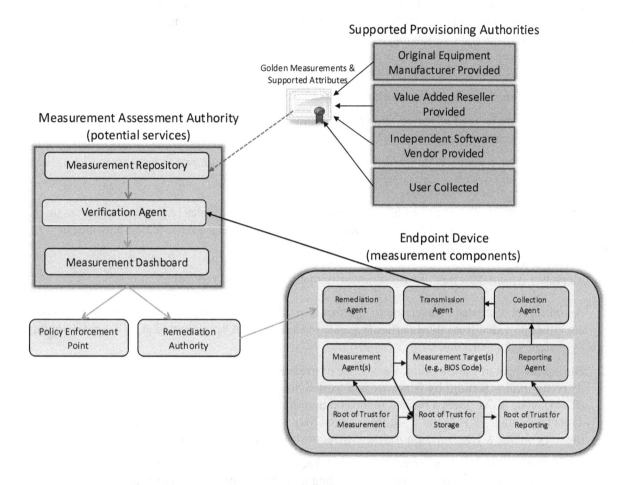

Figure 1: BIOS Integrity Architecture

The BIOS code and configuration data represent the measurement target. The Measurement generation and Reporting Agents act on the measurement target and directly leverage the roots of trust to provide security protection for the individual measurements and for the measurement and reporting processes. Sections 3.2 and 3.3 provide more insight into both the measurements and associated processes. The Collection and Transmission Agents provide a means of reliably collecting and transmitting the measurements to a Measurement Assessment Authority (MAA) for further analysis. Sections 3.4 and 3.5 discuss functions of these agents. The Remediation Agent discussed in Section 3.6 provides a means for an administrative authority to take action to remedy any issues with the endpoint discovered through the analysis of the BIOS measurements.

In assessing the measurements, the MAA references a set of characteristics. These sets come in two varieties: either endpoint attributes and measurements of BIOS code provided and vouched for (using certificates) by the Original Equipment Manufacturer (OEM), Value Added Reseller (VAR), or an Independent Software Vendor (ISV), or measurements of configuration settings gathered by the user/administrator of the endpoint during initial provisioning of the endpoint or the MAA. The assemblage of ideal measurement characteristics is referred to as *golden measurements*.

The MAA may host a number of services, such as a management console or dashboard that provides an easy user interface to the analysis of BIOS attributes and measurements, allowing an administrator or analyst to quickly determine the following:

- The trustworthiness of the endpoint device reports

- If machines are compliant (match the current set of golden measurements)

- If machines are in need of remediation (BIOS settings are out of compliance or older golden measurements are in use)

- If machines are potentially dangerous (certain measurements are known to indicate malicious activity)

Based on these reports, machines can be allowed or denied access to resources (e.g., allowed access to network resources, allowed restricted access to network resources, such as a remediation network, or denied access), or the reports could trigger other administrative actions.

Figure 1 depicts a typical data flow for BIOS integrity measurement and reporting:

1. An initial set of trusted measurements (golden measurements) is obtained. These measurements are either provided from third parties (e.g., OEM) to the MAA or generated at initial provisioning by system administrators.

2. During the boot of the endpoint, a sequence of measurements is made of the BIOS firmware and its configuration settings by firmware in a trust chain rooted in a Root of Trust for Measurement (RTM). The RTM stores a hashed representation of these is stored or protected by the Root of Trust for Storage (RTS), and a log from which they can be reconstructed is stored somewhere in memory so that a Transmission Agent may reconstruct the measurements.

3. In response to an action by either the endpoint requesting a service or an MAA request, the MAA generates a request for measurements, including a random nonce. The Transmission Agent receives this request, determines that it pertains to BIOS Integrity Measurements, and therefore passes it on to the Collection Agent.

4. The Collection Agent parses the request and passes the nonce to the Reporting Agent, which uses the Root of Trust for Reporting to obtain a signature of the nonce and the stored hash representation of the measurements.

5. The Reporting Agent passes that data (along with the log retrieved from memory) back to the Collection Agent.

6. The Collection Agent formats this data in a standard format and passes it back to the Transmission Agent.

7. The Transmission Agent transmits the data to the MAA's Verification Agent.

8. The Verification Agent verifies the signature over the hashes by verifying both the public key used to sign them and the signature itself, and that the nonce contained in the report matches the nonce sent in the request for measurements. It then compares those signed measurements with the golden measurements it obtained earlier.

9. Results of that comparison, collated with other such comparisons from other machines may be displayed via a user interface (such as a management console or dashboard) to the administrator and/or provided to an automated enforcement/access point.

10. If the results are provided to an automated enforcement/access point, the administrator or his proxy then makes a decision pursuant to the results of the comparison, which may be to allow or deny network access, send a signal to a Remediation Agent, or possibly send a service technician to the machine to determine the reason for an erroneous result.

2.3   Transitioning to the Desired State

In the desired, or objective, state for BIM, measurement of BIOS is part of routine and automated client scanning. As organizations progress from where they are today to the desired state, several steps must be taken. Initially the measurements will only be collected and stored along with other endpoint health data. This data will then be reviewed and analyzed on a regular basis to develop an understanding of the baseline behavior of client BIOS within the organization. Anomalies will be investigated and manually remediated. As dashboard suites and other operational tools are updated to incorporate BIOS integrity information as first order data, the sideline activity and responsibility for BIM can be transitioned to the standard IT operations team. Over time, this will become simply another standard offering of IT services.

3. BIM Functional Components

The following sections provide a description and associated requirement guidelines for the BIM functional components:

- Section 3.1 addresses Roots of Trust (RoTs).

- Section 3.2 defines the establishment of BIOS integrity attribute and measurement baselines.

- Section 3.3 addresses BIOS integrity reporting.

- Section 3.4 defines the collection and transmission of BIMs to the MAA.

- Section 3.5 describes and defines the requirements for the MAA itself.

- Section 3.6 addresses potential remediation actions based on the collected and transmitted measurements and attributes.

3.1 Roots of Trust (RoTs)

Roots of Trust (RoTs) are at the foundation of any BIOS integrity assurance. *RoTs* are components (software, hardware, or hybrid) and computing engines that constitute a set of unconditionally trusted functions, and that must always behave in an expected manner because their misbehavior cannot be detected. They are particularly critical for BIOS integrity measurement since the BIOS is generally responsible for the configuration of the software execution environment, including the mapping of physical memory and devices.

The trustworthiness of Software Agents that leverage one or more RoTs is dependent on the trustworthiness of the RoT itself and its attack surface. The complete set of RoTs has at least the minimum set of capabilities to enable the measurement, storage, and reporting of the endpoint characteristics that affect the endpoint's trustworthiness. A Hardware RoT is preferred over a Software RoT since it can be demonstrated to behave in an expected manner in a significantly higher percentage of attack scenarios.

Reliable and trustworthy BIOS integrity measurement and reporting depend upon Software Agents to perform functions upon which a verifier must rely. Each Software Agent relies upon RoTs and the level of trustworthiness in the Agent depends on its RoTs. The RoT for any Software Agent is the computing engine either capable of reliably and accurately performing that Agent's functions, or responsible for reliably spawning Software Agents to perform the task. As such, an Agent may be implemented entirely within the RoT or may be spawned by its RoT via a trusted chain anchored in the RoT. Therefore, the trustworthiness of the Agent is dependent on its respective RoT and trust chain.

The highest-assurance mechanisms for BIOS integrity measurement provide mutable state tolerance, where the mechanisms are able to provide reliable and trustworthy reports on the BIOS and its configuration, irrespective of the overall machine configuration or the contents of the BIOS storage device. In addition, the highest-assurance mechanisms for BIOS integrity measurement provide memory disclosure tolerance, where measurements reported by the mechanisms must be provably fresh (i.e., recently taken, generally for a specific request) and not spoofed by any party, even with full knowledge of all contents ever present in software-readable memory throughout all past software execution. Thus, such mechanisms are more robust against exploits of software vulnerabilities, and are not affected by disclosure of cryptographic keys present in software-readable memory.

3.1.1 Overview of Software Agents

BIM requires the coordination of a Measurement Agent to harvest measurements, a Storage Agent to protect the measurements from modification until they can be reported, and a Reporting Agent to reliably report the measurements. If the measurements are reported immediately after harvesting, there may not be a need to use a Storage Agent. A comprehensive system for ensuring BIOS integrity will also include some form of verification of the collected measurements, and correspondingly will utilize Verification Agents that assess reported measurements. Such Verification Agents may be resident on the measured endpoint, or may reside externally in the management services or infrastructure. In addition, if any Software Agents can be modified or updated, then the trustworthiness of such Agents depends upon the mechanism used to implement updates. Thus, if such updates are possible, the endpoint should include Update Agents to effect software updates in a reliable manner providing protections equivalent to [NIST-SP800-147].

3.1.2 Overview of Roots of Trust

The *RoT for Measurement (RTM)* is a computing engine capable of making inherently reliable integrity measurements. It is the root of the chain of transitive trust for subsequent Measurement Agents. A small RTM applied very soon after a re-initialization of an endpoint may have greater value than an RTM instantiated later, mainly in minimizing the attack surface's exposure to subversion of the measurement process. The later the endpoint invokes the RTM, the more opportunity an adversary has to subvert the measurement trust chain. The larger the RTM, the greater the chance that a flaw in its implementation will provide an opportunity for an adversary to subvert the RTM.

The *RoT for Storage (RTS)* is a computing engine capable of maintaining a tamper-evident summary of integrity measurement values and the sequence of those measurements. It does not include the details of the sequence of integrity measurements, but rather holds integrity hashes for those sequences. These integrity hashes can either be used to verify the integrity of a log containing the integrity measurement values and the sequence of those measurements, or it can be used as a proxy for that log. The RTS maintains these integrity hashes in tamper-evident locations. For example, the interface may allow register extensions (defined in Section 3.2.2.2) but disallow direct register writes. These authorized interfaces are commonly called *protected capabilities*. Together the tamper-evident locations and protected capabilities collectively form the RTS.

The *RoT for Reporting (RTR)* is a computing engine capable of reliably reporting information provided by the RTM and its Measurement Agent(s) or held by the RTS. The RTR serves as the basis for the capabilities of integrity and non-repudiation of reports of measurement data. It necessarily leverages the RTM and RTS. A key requirement for the RTR is an unambiguous identity, both of the endpoint and the components being measured and reported. This identity may be persistent or temporary. Signatures of measurement report data using keys are a common mechanism to provide unambiguous identity. Certificates for keys may certify membership in a group or identify a particular member.

3.1.3 Agent Coordination

The trustworthiness of the coordination of all of the relevant Agents in combination gives Verification Agents the confidence to make a reliable assessment of the BIOS integrity of measured endpoints. Evaluation of the trust properties afforded by the composed system is critical, and evaluation of an individual Agent's trust properties is only relevant in the context of the entire system.

Figure 2 illustrates that the RoTs must act in concert and build on each other to enable reliable and trustworthy measurement, reporting, and verification of BIMs. In addition, these RoTs must properly integrate with mechanisms for integrity protection and authentication for secure BIOS updates. The implementation of these RoTs, and other endpoint security mechanisms, may be achieved in an integrated fashion, where all are comprised within a single software component, such as the BIOS. Whether the implementation is monolithic or disaggregated, the combination of these RoTs, and the combination of the RoTs that they are built upon, forms the basis for the trustworthiness of the total BIM solution.

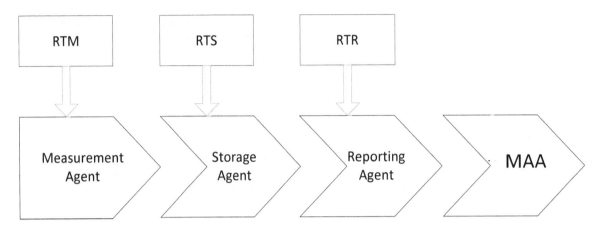

Figure 2: Coordination of RoTs and Agents

3.1.4 Security Guidelines for RoTs

1. The endpoint vendor SHALL provide the hardware support necessary to implement credible RTMs, RTSs, and RTRs and use that support to implement corresponding RoTs for BIMs.

2. The endpoint vendor SHALL combine the mechanisms of the RTM, RTS, and RTR to form an integrated, reliable foundation for BIMs.

3. The endpoint vendor SHOULD provide mechanisms for integrity-protected, non-bypassable implementation of authenticated or secure BIOS updates, as necessary to conform to [NIST-SP800-147].

4. The endpoint vendor MAY provide hardware support for implementing a credible dynamic RTM for post boot-time measurements. The endpoint vendor and OS vendor MAY use that support to implement such an RoT for BIMs.

3.2 Integrity Attribute and Measurement Baselines

A key factor in a meaningful integrity measurement comparison scheme is establishing and maintaining, with confidence, a known baseline of attributes and measurements with which one can make decisions. The establishment of a baseline must take into account two scenarios: endpoint devices with a BIOS of unknown or questionable provenance, and endpoint devices with a known and trusted (protected and signed) BIOS. This section lists attributes and measurements for the baselines.

3.2.1 Overview of BIOS Integrity Attributes

Attributes are used for assessing confidence in BIOS integrity measurements. Endpoint vendors have various ways to convey attributes to users. The endpoint vendor may present these attributes along with golden BIOS measurements in a certificate to the user in an out-of-band channel (i.e., not delivered with the endpoint itself, but through other means). The endpoint vendor may allow the user to query the endpoint and extract the attributes directly. Alternatively, the endpoint vendor may allow the user to present a serial number to a managed online service, which then responds with a list of attributes for the endpoint as it was delivered. Regardless of how the user obtains the attributes for a particular endpoint, the reason for the attributes is to give the user a means of assessing the validity of the BIMs reported by the endpoint and developing a level of confidence in the reports it receives about the overall health status of the endpoint beyond only the BIMs.

3.2.1.1 List of BIOS Integrity Attributes

This section lists BIOS integrity attributes and suggests possible values for them.

1. **RTM** - The attribute of the RTM provides information about the amount of time/code available to the adversary before measurement of the BIOS takes place, often referred to as the size of the attack surface. The sooner an endpoint can leverage an RTM and take BIOS measurements, the smaller the attack surface, and the more confidence an assessor can have in the measurements. The later in time after initialization or re-initialization an endpoint leverage an RTM before taking BIOS measurements, the larger the attack surface and the less confidence an assessor may have in the measurements. Examples of the values for an attribute of an RTM include:

   - Class 1 (i.e., the endpoint instantiates the RTM as part of the early BIOS POST initialization)

   - Class 2 (i.e., the endpoint instantiates the RTM after the early BIOS POST initialization)

2. **RTS** - The attribute of the RTS provides information about the protections afforded for tamper-evident locations. The more likely an RTS is to rebuff attacks from an adversary, the more confidence an assessor can have in the measurements it contains. The values for the RTS may take on the following:

   - Class 1: Hardware-based (e.g., TPM 1.2, processor-based protected storage)

   - Class 2: Software-based (e.g., OS key store, System Management Random Access Memory (SMRAM))

3. **RTR** - The attribute of the RTR provides information about the protections afforded to the data to be reported, the keying material used to provide authentication, the code using the key for signatures, and non-repudiation services. The more likely an RTR is to rebuff attacks from an adversary, the more confidence an assessor can have in the reports. The values for an RTR attribute may include:

   - Class 1: Hardware-based (e.g., TPM 1.2, processor-based)

   - Class 2: Software-based (e.g., OS, BIOS Boot Block + Key stored in BIOS)

4. **BIOS Signature Present** - This is an indication of whether or not the BIOS has been signed and the signatures are present with the BIOS. Values include:

   - None (none of the BIOS is signed)

   - Partial (some of the BIOS components are signed and present)

   - Full (All BIOS components have been signed and the signatures are present)

5. **BIOS Update Mechanisms** - This attribute provides an indication of the type of BIOS update mechanism employed by the vendor. The importance of this attribute lies in the diligence exercised by the BIOS provider in providing the latest update of the BIOS code and data provided. In the context of security, the presence of a reliable BIOS mechanism provides the end user with assurance that the BIOS provider can safely remediate their products against threats

should the need arise. A BIOS with an unreliable or nonexistent update mechanism may be held in suspicion. Values include:

- None (it's not possible to update the BIOS)

- Capsule (from OS, write new BIOS to RAM, then perform a system reboot)

- System Management Mode (SMM) (from OS, use SMM to modify the BIOS, then continue without rebooting the system; reboot is necessary for realization of new BIOS)

- Other

6. **Virtualization** - This attribute provides an indication of whether the BIOS originates from the endpoint hardware or is provided as part of a virtual machine (VM). Values include:

- None (physical BIOS present)

- Full (virtual BIOS in play)

7. **Flash Lockdown** - This attribute provides an indication of the capability of the endpoint to protect the flash where the BIOS resides from unauthorized modification. This term normally refers to a hardware capability. The importance of this attribute lies in the diligence exercised by the BIOS provider in providing protections against unauthorized modifications of the BIOS code and data. In the context of security, the presence of reliable BIOS flash protection provides the end user with confidence in the BIOS measurements. A BIOS with unreliable or nonexistent flash protections may be held in suspicion. Values include:

- None

- Chipset

- Native to flash chip

3.2.1.2 Security Guidelines for RoT Attributes

1. Endpoint vendors SHALL provide the attributes defined in Section 3.2.1.1.

2. Endpoint vendors SHALL provide reference measurements of executable BIOS boot code at the lowest level of granularity for which they provide update and maintenance and that can be used to verify measurements returned from the RTR.

3. Endpoint vendors SHALL provide a mechanism for measuring and reporting a baseline of measurements for BIOS configuration data.

4. Endpoint vendors SHOULD deploy BIOS measurement and reporting mechanisms that do not preclude extension to option ROMs external to the system BIOS.

5. Endpoint vendors SHOULD provide attributes in a standardized format.

6. Endpoint vendors MAY provide an indication of compliance with [NIST-SP800-147].

3.2.2 Overview of BIOS Integrity Measurements

This section defines the minimal essential BIMs all endpoints are to be capable of reporting. It addresses the format of these measurements and how they are generated.

BIOS Boot Code Integrity Measurement - The BIOS boot code integrity measurement is either a cryptographic hash of the BIOS boot code or an extended cryptographic hash of the BIOS boot code modules. In either case, it can simply be referred to as "the hash". The hash includes the following components if implemented:

- BIOS boot block
- SMM code
- Advanced Configuration and Power Interface (ACPI) code
- Power On Self Test (POST) code
- BIOS recovery mechanism code
- BIOS update mechanism code
- BBM software
- RTM
- Embedded Option ROMs (those Option ROMs embedded in the BIOS boot code and controlled by the BIOS vendor)

BIOS Configuration Data Integrity Measurements - The BIOS configuration data integrity measurement is either a cryptographic hash of the user configurable data components of the BIOS, or an extended cryptographic hash of the individual configuration data components. All such BIOS configuration data must be measured, with the exception of endpoint configuration information that is automatically updated, such as clock registers, and system unique information, such as asset numbers or serial numbers. These must not be measured into the same register. If measured, system unique information, such as asset numbers, serial numbers, password hashes, etc. should be measured into a different privacy register. This allows for a consistent measurement to be established both among identical systems and between boot measurements of the same system, but also allows a system administrator to determine if passwords have been changed.

In practice, live integrity measurements of BIOS components taken from various endpoints of the same make and model produce distinct and unique values. This seems counterintuitive, especially for integrity measurements of static BIOS components. The absence of golden BIOS measurements makes further investigation problematic, especially in distinguishing between compromised and authentic BIOSes.

In practice, RoTs maintain composites of BIMs. Although specifications recommend how individual integrity measurements should be stored and preserved, the lack of standardization makes interpretation of these measurements for forensics problematic.

3.2.2.1 BIOS Integrity Measurement Generation and Storage

In order to monitor and improve BIOS integrity, BIOS integrity measurements must start being securely generated and stored. These measurements can then be transmitted, analyzed, reported on, and used to provide remediation. This section describes how endpoints generate and store BIMs.

The endpoint RTM must serve as the anchor for the chain of trust for measurement. The endpoint forms a chain of trust for measurement by having the endpoint RTM measure one or more binary components and recording those measurement(s) in a safe place before the binary component(s) executes. In turn, the endpoint maintains the chain of trust for measurement by delegating measurement to only those components measured either by the endpoint RTM or by some other component whose measurement can be traced back to the endpoint RTM. The chain of trust for measurement should measure all BIOS configuration data (non-executable binaries) prior to the endpoint consuming it.

3.2.2.2 BIOS Integrity Measurement Registers

For clarity, this document creates and uses a number of "register" types. The term register is meant to explain the various types of storage capabilities needed and how they are used, not to define any particular implementation architecture or naming convention.

As the trust chain for measurement measures BIOS code and data, the endpoint must store the measurements in a trusted place that would accommodate later monitoring and inspection should the administrator of the endpoint desire it. The endpoint RTM and the chain of trust for measurement store the measurements in Integrity Measurement Registers (IMRs) contained in the RTS. They will hash BIOS components (code and data) using an approved cryptographic hash algorithm such as one of those published in [NIST-FIPS180-3]. The IMRs should be of sufficient length to accommodate the entire result of the hash chosen from the approved list.

BIOS integrity measurement implementers SHALL initialize each IMR to a known fixed value. They may hash all the BIOS components intended for a register together at once and extend the result in a BIOS IMR. Alternatively, implementers may create a composite of hashes by serially hashing BIOS components one at a time and extending the BIOS code IMR in the following way for each component:

$IMR_{new} = H(IMR_{old}||H(BIOS_{component}))$

IMR_{new} is the new IMR

IMR_{old} is the old value of the IMR

$BIOS_{component}$ is the BIOS component to be measured

H is a hash algorithm from the approved list

$||$ is the concatenation operator

It is OPTIONAL to use a keyed hash algorithm, such as HMAC, when measuring BIOS components. A randomized hash algorithm MAY be applied for additional collision resistance, such as the one published in [NIST-SP800-106]. In that case, the size of the IMRs MUST accommodate the output of the randomized hash algorithms, along with the additional parameters necessary to verify the hashes.

The endpoint SHALL initialize the IMRs to a known fixed value before measurement of any BIOS component takes place. Ideally, power-on of the endpoint initializes these registers. Only an endpoint reset which causes the BIOS to fully execute SHOULD cause the reset of these registers. An endpoint recovering from the invocation of suspension (commonly called sleep and hibernation modes) will not initialize IMRs, but rather restore valid values saved during the suspension process.

The endpoint accumulates all measurements of BIOS executable components together into one IMR. Likewise, the endpoint performs the same process for all measurements of BIOS configuration data components, with the exception of privacy sensitive data, such as passwords, serial numbers, asset numbers, keying material, etc. and elements such as time which make golden measurements impossible. These excluded items tend to be unique to platforms and could cause platforms that administrators have configured identically to project different configuration data IMRs. Also, since these items are privacy sensitive, administrators may want the option to configure the measurement and reporting of these values. The endpoint SHALL accumulate BIOS executable code measurements in the BIOS code integrity measurement register (CIMR), SHALL accumulate BIOS data measurements in the BIOS data integrity measurement register (DIMR), and SHOULD accumulate BIOS privacy sensitive data in the BIOS privacy integrity measurement register (PIMR).

3.2.2.3 BIOS Measurement Log

In addition to extending BIOS code and data measurements into the CIMR and DIMR, respectively, BIOS functions MAY also extend optional measurements and events into them. To aid in disentangling the measurements placed in the register, an administrator would find great value in a log that describes the measurements and events extended into them. Several examples include:

- The endpoint vendor maintains and updates BIOS code in modules, and programs the BIOS code to measure and extend the CIMR on a module by module basis. A log would help an MAA detect the cases in which one or more bad or unanticipated measurements were extended into the CIMR.

- If the endpoint contains more than one BIOS image, e.g. an operational and a backup, an administrator may want to gain additional details about which copy was measured and extended into the CIMR. An early stage BIOS function may extend an "event" into the CIMR that signals the choice taken, along with a corresponding entry in the log.

- The BIOS may want to "cap" measurement extensions just before handing off execution to a post-boot environment. By extending a "cap" event into the CIMR or DIMR and recording a corresponding event in the log, an administrator can detect which events occurred during which phase of the endpoint initialization.

- BIOS configuration data has many permutations. An event log recording measurements and events involving BIOS configuration data, if formatted appropriately, could aid in a programmatic review for unanticipated changes.

A stored measurement log (SML) allows higher endpoint agents, such as the Reporting and Collection Agents, to gather them for preprocessing and correlation before forwarding to an MAA. Since these agents typically run in a post-boot environment, the BIOS SHOULD take care in preserving the contents of the SML during the handoff to a new environment.

SML measurements typically have better granularity than CIMR or DIMR values, but do not have the finest granularity of containing the raw BIOS firmware or configuration data. While a system SHALL have SML data available for reporting, it SHOULD provide a means to programmatically report and interpret the BIOS configuration data. The TCG provides a standard format for SML log entries in [TCG-ConvBiosSpec].

3.2.2.4 Security Guidelines for BIOS Integrity Measurement Generation and Storage

1. Measured Components

    a. The endpoint SHALL measure all BIOS executable components.

    b. The endpoint SHALL measure all BIOS configuration data components, with the exception of privacy sensitive data.

    c. The endpoint SHOULD measure privacy sensitive data separate from other BIOS configuration data components.

2. BIOS Measurement Generation and Storage

    a. The endpoint SHALL support boot-time measurement.

    b. The endpoint SHALL use an RTM or a component in the chain of trust for measurement rooted in an RTM to generate BIOS integrity measurements.

    c. The endpoint SHALL use approved standard cryptographic techniques to generate BIOS integrity measurements.

    d. The endpoint SHALL use standard BIOS integrity measurements formats.

    e. The format and reporting of BIMs – both golden measurements and endpoint measurements – SHALL use open standards or specifications, such as [TCG-Manifest] and [TCG-Integrity].

    f. The endpoint vendor SHOULD use an extensible system to enable adding support for measuring option ROMs, etc.

    g. The endpoint SHALL store BIMs in an RTS.

    h. The endpoint vendor SHOULD make raw BIOS configuration data available for reporting and SHOULD have a means of interpretation of that data available.

3. Measurement Log

    a. BIOS functions SHALL record in an SML measurement and event extensions into the CIMR and DIMR.

    b. BIOS functions SHOULD record in an SML measurement and event extensions into the PIMR.

    c. BIOS functions SHALL use a standardized format, such as [TCG-ConvBiosSpec], when recording BIM and other BIOS-related events in an SML.

    d. BIOS SHALL ensure the proper handoff of the SML to the post-boot environment.

4. Measurement Support

    a. The OS vendor SHALL support a standard application programming interface (API) for collecting measurements.

    b. The endpoint, OS, and application vendors SHALL support an RTR for collecting and reporting BIMs.

3.2.2.5 Relevant Standards and Specifications

There are several standards of note related to these requirements. The [NIST-SP800-147] specification spells out the necessary conditions for achieving and maintaining an immutable BIOS boot block upon which an RTM depends. The [TCG-ConvBiosSpec] specification defines for which BIOS components the RTM (i.e., BIOS) should take measurements and store them in the RTS (e.g., TPM). The TCG EFI Platform Specification Version 1.20 Revision 1.0 [TCG-EFI] specifies the Extensible Firmware Interface (EFI) components that the RTM, or by extension the chain of trust within the EFI, should measure and store in the RTS (e.g., TPM). Finally, the TCG Infrastructure Working Group Reference Manifest Schema Specification Version 1.0 [TCG-Manifest] specifies the format which vendors can use to report BIOS integrity golden measurements, endpoint measurements, and BIOS integrity measurement attributes.

3.3 BIOS Integrity Reporting

Reporting of the BIOS integrity values stored in the RTS is performed by an Endpoint Reporting Agent.

3.3.1 Endpoint Reporting Agent

The endpoint RTR and the Reporting Agent anchored in the RTR are responsible for extracting the measurements stored in the IMRs of the RTS. It is critical that the RTR and the Reporting Agent apply integrity and non-repudiation protections on the data so that subsequent agents cannot alter or replace the data without detection by the MAA. In addition, unambiguous identity is an important property to apply to the data so that the MAA knows the source of the data. Typically a signature over the data using a key recognized by the MAA is sufficient to satisfy the integrity, non-repudiation, and unambiguous identity goals.

In addition the Reporting Agent is responsible for supplying the SML corresponding to the IMR data. It is desirable to identify the components measured based on a component ID that uniquely identifies the manufacturer, model, and version, thus allowing the MAA to compare the measurements against its golden measurements.

The endpoint Reporting Agent is given a nonce which originates in the MAA and is passed to it through the Transmission Agent and Collection Agent. It then passes this nonce to the RTR and receives back a signature over the nonce together with the hash representation of the measurements stored in the RTS. It also obtains the SML and puts the two together in a standard format. This report must eventually be readable by an MAA. Therefore

1. The defined report format SHALL use [TCG-Integrity].

2. The report SHOULD contain a copy of the BIOS configuration, in an industry standard format, if the ability to parse and determine the acceptability of the configuration is desired.

In addition to the above guidance and the standards listed throughout Section 3.3, the requirements below in Section 3.3.2 apply to the BIOS measurement reports that are provided to the Verification Agent in the MAA.

3.3.2 Security Guidelines for the Reporting Protocol

1. BIOS reporting mechanisms MAY prepare and issue a BIOS integrity report to an authenticated MAA upon any of the following conditions:

   a. When a change was made to the BIOS configuration

   b. When a change was made to the BIOS software

   c. When a local port was used to access the BIOS or its configuration

   d. When a BIOS error condition has been generated

   e. Upon connection to a network controlled by an authenticated MAA.

2. BIOS reporting mechanisms MAY support the ability to configure specific events to trigger reports of BIOS integrity measurements.

3. Report requests MAY be initiated by either the reporter or the receiver of the report. The following requirements apply to requests that are initiated by either side:

   a. Mechanisms SHALL be capable of providing provably fresh BIOS reports that are sent to the MAA.

   b. The report SHOULD include a reference to the formatting standard/schema used for the report.

   c. The report format SHOULD include a version field that can be updated over time as the report format gets extended or otherwise changes.

   d. All requests to issue or provide a report from an unauthenticated entity SHOULD be ignored.

e. Requests to provide or issue a report MAY contain a priority that indicates the urgency of the request.

f. Response timeframes related to requests MAY be configurable by the licensed user based on priority.

3.3.3 Relevant Standards and Specifications

BIOS measurements need to be provided in a standard schema so that they can be used and acted upon by the receiving entity based on policy. Therefore, the following standards and guidance should be employed for establishing a trust model for reporting and for providing standard reporting formats and transport for BIOS measurements.

The TCG Infrastructure Working Group Integrity Report Schema Specification [TCG-Integrity] defines the structure with which integrity information is communicated between entities. The TCG Trusted Network Connect (TNC) Working Group IF-M Specification [TCG-IF-M] defines a protocol for an MAA to request measurements from an endpoint, and for the endpoint to provide those measurements to the MAA.

The TCG Trusted Network Connect Architecture for Interoperability specification [TCG-ARCH-INTER] describes an open solution architecture that enables network operators to enforce policies regarding the security state of endpoints in order to determine whether to grant access to a requested network infrastructure. Endpoint integrity policies may involve integrity parameters spanning a range of system components (hardware, firmware, software, and application settings), and may or may not include evidence of a TPM. This security assessment of each endpoint is performed using a set of asserted integrity measurements covering aspects of the operational environment of the endpoint. IF-M, IF-TNCCS, and IF-T are key TNC protocols for transmitting measurements from an endpoint to an MAA.

NIST IR 7802 [NIST-IR-7802] provides recommendations on how to use existing specifications to represent signatures, hashes, key information, and identity information in the context of an XML document within the security automation domain. NIST IR 7694 [NIST-IR-7694] describes the Asset Reporting Format (ARF), a data model for expressing the transport format of information about assets and the relationships between assets and reports. The standardized data model facilitates the reporting, correlating, and fusing of asset information throughout and between organizations. NIST SP 800-126 [NIST-SP800-126] defines the Security Content Automation Protocol (SCAP), a suite of specifications that standardize the format and nomenclature by which security software products communicate security content, particularly software flaw and security configuration information. SCAP is a multi-purpose protocol that supports automated configuration, vulnerability, and patch checking, technical control compliance activities, and security measurement.

The DMTF's System Management BIOS (SMBIOS) Reference Specification [DMTF-SMBIOS] addresses how motherboard and system vendors present management information about their products in a standard format by extending the BIOS interface on x86 architecture systems. This specification is intended to provide enough information that BIOS developers may implement the necessary extensions to allow the hardware on their products and other system-related information to be accurately determined by users of the defined interfaces. In addition, in cases where the implementer has provided write access to non-volatile storage on the system, some information may be updated by management applications after a system is deployed in the field to record data that persists between system starts. The specification is also intended to provide enough information for developers of management instrumentation to develop generic routines for translating from SMBIOS format to the format used by their chosen management technology, whether it is a DMTF technology like DMI or CIM, or another technology. To support this translation for DMTF technologies, sections of this specification describe the DMI groups and CIM classes intended to convey the information retrieved from an SMBIOS-compatible system through the interfaces described in the document.

Finally, the TCG Attestation PTS Protocol: Binding to TNC IF-M specification [TCG-Att-PTS] and the TCG Infrastructure Working Group Integrity Report Schema Specification [TCG-Integrity] define how to use IF to request and send Integrity Reports. They also adds the means to send the random nonce and support TLV-based integrity report data.

3.4 BIOS Integrity Measurement Collection and Transmission

3.4.1 Overview of Measurement Collection and Transmission

BIMs are collected and placed in a standard format by the Collection Agent, then transmitted from the endpoint to the MAA by a Transmission Agent. This section describes the requirements that must be met by the Collection Agent and Transmission Agent.

Secure transmission of BIMs ensures that measurements are not modified, disclosed, or forged in transit by malicious parties. Further, proper selection of transmission protocols should ensure maximum interoperability, freshness, and efficiency. In addition, cryptographic protection of the integrity and source authentication of measurements starting at the RTR ensures that even if the Collection Agent, Transmission Agent, or other software becomes compromised, the measurements cannot be falsified.

3.4.2 Security Guidelines for Measurement Collection and Transmission

The Transmission Agent SHALL securely transmit measurements of BIOS integrity from endpoints to the MAA, as follows:

1. All reporting sessions SHALL:
   a. have the ability to provide confidentiality protection.
   b. provide integrity protection and freshness.
   c. authenticate the MAA.
   d. provide authentication of endpoint identities.
2. The Transmission Agent:
   a. SHALL permit measurements to be integrity protected all the way from the RTR to the verifying component.
   b. SHOULD support a variety of different services such as continuous monitoring, network access control, and application-layer integrity monitoring
   c. SHOULD ensure the resulting system is inexpensive, unobtrusive, high performance, and secure (although higher levels of security may require higher levels of cost)
3. Collection Agents and Transmission Agents on endpoints SHOULD support open standards that enable interoperability among many different kinds of endpoints and MAAs over many different forms of communications media, to the extent that such standards are available.

3.4.3 Relevant Standards and Specifications

There are several standards relevant to the above requirements. The PA-TNC specification [IETF-RFC-5792] is equivalent to TCG's IF-M 1.0 [TCG-IF-M]; it describes a standard structure for requesting and transmitting integrity measurements. The PB-TNC specification [IETF-RFC-5793] is equivalent to TCG's IF-TNCCS 2.0. It describes a standard protocol for conducting an integrity measurement exchange. The TCG Trusted Network Connect TNC IF-T: Binding to TLS specification [TCG-IF-T-TLS] describes how an integrity measurement exchange is transmitted over the TLS protocol, after network connectivity has been established. The TCG Trusted Network Connect TNC IF-T: Protocol Bindings for Tunneled EAP Methods specification [TCG-IF-T-EAP] describes how an integrity measurement exchange is transmitted over EAP, before network connectivity has been established. Finally, the TCG Attestation PTS Protocol: Binding to TNC IF-M specification [TCG-Att-PTS] defines how to use IF to request and send Integrity Reports. It also adds the means to send the random nonce and support TLV-based integrity report data.

3.5 Measurement Assessment Authority

3.5.1 Overview

The MAA is responsible for several things. It transmits a nonce to the client Transmission Agent to guarantee it will receive fresh measurements back from the client. It receives the transmission from the client Transmission Agent in response, which will consist of a report detailing the BIMs together with a signature over the nonce and a set of hashes which together prove the integrity of that report.

When these items are reliably and robustly reported, it allows an enterprise management system to accurately determine the state of the security relevant BIOS configuration items on the system. With this information, the MAA can report on and act upon the specific configuration items with which the organization is concerned. It is not forced to act only upon the fact that a change in some unspecified configuration item has caused the overall measurement to deviate from its last recorded value, when the configuration item that changed may not even be security relevant. It should be possible for the administrative component of the BIOS reporting mechanism to select which attributes are reported. For individual BIOS configuration items, a security administrator can be expected to provide the desired values for items which are of concern to the organization.

Collected and reported BIOS measurements can be used to make an access decision, either through quarantine, denial of access to network resources or remediation. It also provides situational awareness of one aspect of a network's security posture based on the integrity of the devices on the network. The adoption of TCG-compliant BIOS by endpoint vendors will provide some of the necessary infrastructure to reliably establish, measure, and report the state of the BIOS on endpoints. At a minimum, the MAA has to be able to provide the state of the system either for display to an IT administrator or to an automated access/enforcement point. Information collected may be reported to a policy enforcement/decision point for some form of remediation or response, or may be fed to visualization capabilities that provide a network operator or analyst with an aggregated and normalized view of the integrity of the assets on a network. Visualization/situational awareness capabilities exist today that collect other device measurements; the addition of BIOS integrity measurements is a natural and straightforward extension.

The BIOS may be subject to *bit rot*, or modifications where the bits of the BIOS contents may change spuriously as a result of random faults as determined by the physical properties of the BIOS storage device hardware. Depending on the BIOS storage device hardware, those spurious modifications may happen with some frequency in very large installations; as a result, unexpected BIOS measurements may be reported potentially weekly or daily. To avoid the assumption that all unexpected measurements are due to bit rot, and to facilitate correct decisions and appropriate actions by operators, the MAA MAY provide mechanisms that allow assessing whether measurement results are likely due to bit rot.

3.5.2 Security Guidelines for the MAA

1. The MAA SHALL be capable of storing expected values (golden measurements).

2. The MAA SHALL be capable of comparing new reported values against expected values and/or previously reported (last known) measurements.

3. The MAA SHALL be capable of storing reported values.

4. MAAs SHALL support open standards that enable interoperability among many different kinds of endpoints and MAAs over many different forms of communications media, to the extent that such standards are available.

5. The MAA MAY be capable of providing an assessment of the likelihood that an unexpected, anomalous measurement is the result of a bit rot, if provided with the contents of the BIOS that generated the anomalous measurement as well as the BIOS contents for which golden measurements exist.

3.6 Remediation Activities

Remediation is the process of correcting a problem with a computing system. In the context of BIOS security, remediation refers to actions such as upgrading an outdated BIOS to a known-good version and reconfiguring a BIOS to meet an organization's security requirements. There are often several options for the processes used to remediate a BIOS security problem. The appropriate process option or options for each case may vary according to several factors, including the type of problem (BIOS update, configuration change, etc.), the nature of the problem (intentional attack versus accidental change), the relative importance of the system, and the organization's incident handling policies and practices. Each organization needs to determine which factors are relevant for their environment and determine how to incorporate them into remediation activities. Further discussion of this is outside the scope of this publication.

The remediation discussion in this section does not take into account incident handling and forensic activities, which are outside the scope of this publication. See NIST SP 800-61 for additional information on incident handling and NIST SP 800-86 for general forensic guidelines.

3.6.1 Quarantine Strategies

Quarantine is the process of virtually "moving" a compromised system from a position of broad network and resource access (or potential access, in the case of a system being joined to a network) to a pool of networked systems whose access is restricted, so that the target system can "do no harm" before remediation is completed. Full quarantine restricts all network access, while partial quarantine allows the system to access some parts of the network, but not more sensitive regions.

Quarantine is intended to be a short-term state. If mitigation is successful, typically the quarantine ends and the system is allowed its regular network access. If mitigation is not successful, it may be appropriate to completely remove the system from service so that an administrator can manually handle the mitigation.

BIM-supporting products can leverage existing standards to support quarantining. The TCG Trusted Network Connect IF-PEP [TCG-IF-PEP] can be used to send commands between the MAA and the enforcement point to support full or partial quarantining. RFC 3576, Dynamic Authorization Extensions to Remote Authentication Dial In User Service [IETF-RFC-3576], can be used to support dynamic authorization, allowing an MAA and enforcement point to retest an endpoint at a later time and potentially take remedial action, including quarantining the system.

3.6.2 Remediation Automation

Organizations may have several options for partially or fully automating their BIOS remediation actions. Different options are appropriate for different situations and environments. For example, one organization may want their BIOS remediation to be completely driven by external systems (e.g., enterprise network and system management), while another organization may want remediation to be completely self-contained in the product, and to have remediation actions performed as soon as possible using fully automated means. There are many approaches between these extremes, with most manufacturers shipping their products with a default automated remediation strategy. Possible strategies include the following:

1. Fully automated, self-contained. In the case of some systems, there may be specialized trusted hardware out of band to the normal system that can provide full remediation to the system in the event of a compromise.

2. Fully automated, externally driven. Most enterprises and large organizations will employ server-based remediation on systems that will allow remote remediation to fix problems. Full reboot will likely be necessary in this case as software by itself is generally not trustable.

3. Partially automated requiring physical operator intervention. For example, if remediation software is compromised, it may be necessary to reboot the system from a secondary source, such as a CD, to employ trusted remediation client software. In any event, the system's operator can be trusted to be involved in the remediation, rather than requiring a trusted IT representative to do it.

4. Partially automated requiring remote owner intervention. In this case an IT representative may have to be dispatched to work on the system rather than its operator.

Products may implement stages of remediation, which include fallback strategies, in the event that initial remediations are unsuccessful. Each stage may be fully automated, may be customer configurable, or may allow for manual intervention. Ordering of remediation stages may similarly be automated or customer configurable. In staged linear remediation, there is a single path of predetermined remediation paths; in staged branching remediation, there is a flexible set of remediation path choice points, based on one or more variable inputs. An example of this would be a server-based remediation that a reboot shows was not successful due to a compromise of the client-based remediation software. At this point, the client can be rebooted to a preboot execution environment (PXE) server, which can then be used to run known-good client-based remediation software, or a technician can be dispatched to the system to remediate it locally.

The PA-TNC specification [IETF-RFC-5792], equivalent to TCG's IF-M 1.0 [TCG-IF-M], can support partially automated remediation that requires physical user intervention on the client. These standards support sending Uniform Resource Identifiers (URIs), such as a web address, or human readable strings from the MAA to the endpoint, to assist the user-driven remediation activity.

The NIST SCAP specifications can also support fully or partially automated remediation activities. Draft NISTIR 7670, Proposed Open Specifications for Enterprise Security Remediation [NIST-IR-7670], examines use cases for enterprise remediation, identifies high-level requirements for these use cases, and proposes a set of emerging specifications that address those requirements.

3.6.3   Restoration Options

There are several possible options for restoring the BIOS software or configuration to a "known good state", including the following:

1. Restoration to manufacturer default configuration

2. Restoration to customer default configuration for general use

3. Restoration to customer default operational configuration for a specific use

4. Restoration to last known good configuration

5. Force the system into a non-operational state (e.g., quarantined, removed from service)

Another consideration for restoration is the policy for handling a system's non-volatile data. Possible options include:

1. No backup

2. Partial backup

3. Full backup

4. Application gating strategy – This strategy can be applied when the compromise is localized to a particular BIOS service that can be selectively disabled.

5. In the event that a particular service (such as a low-level manageability interface) has been compromised, it may be possible to securely turn off the service rather than re-flash the entire BIOS.

3.6.4   Verification Options

After a BIOS has been remediated, an organization may choose to verify its integrity. This usually involves rebooting the system and putting it through its normal test sequence, ensuring that its integrity is restored before giving the system access to network resources. Alternately, an organization may choose to allow systems to return to operation without going through a standard retest. In this case the remediation strategy is trusted at least as much as the trusted measurement that normally takes place upon boot.

Appendix A—Summary of Security Guidelines

This appendix contains a summary of the security guidelines for system BIOS integrity measurement implementations.

Section 3.1.4, Security Guidelines for RoTs

1. The endpoint vendor SHALL provide the hardware support necessary to implement credible RTMs, RTSs, and RTRs and use that support to implement corresponding RoTs for BIMs.

2. The endpoint vendor SHALL combine the mechanisms of the RTM, RTS, and RTR to form an integrated, reliable foundation for BIMs.

3. The endpoint vendor SHOULD provide mechanisms for integrity-protected, non-bypassable implementation of authenticated or secure BIOS updates, as necessary to conform to [NIST-SP800-147].

4. The endpoint vendor MAY provide hardware support for implementing a credible dynamic RTM for post boot-time measurements. The endpoint vendor and OS vendor MAY use that support to implement such an RoT for BIMs.

Section 3.2.1.2, Security Guidelines for RoT Attributes

1. Endpoint vendors SHALL provide the attributes defined in Section 3.2.1.1.

2. Endpoint vendors SHALL provide reference measurements of executable BIOS boot code at the lowest level of granularity for which they provide update and maintenance and that can be used to verify measurements returned from the RTR.

3. Endpoint vendors SHALL provide a mechanism for measuring and reporting a baseline of measurements for BIOS configuration data.

4. Endpoint vendors SHOULD deploy BIOS measurement and reporting mechanisms that do not preclude extension to option ROMs external to the system BIOS.

5. Endpoint vendors SHOULD provide attributes in a standardized format.

6. Endpoint vendors MAY provide an indication of compliance with [NIST-SP800-147].

Section 3.2.2.4, Security Guidelines for BIOS Integrity Measurement Generation and Storage

1. Measured Components

   a. The endpoint SHALL measure all BIOS executable components.

   b. The endpoint SHALL measure all BIOS configuration data components, with the exception of privacy sensitive data.

   c. The endpoint SHOULD measure privacy sensitive data separate from other BIOS configuration data components.

2. BIOS Measurement Generation and Storage

   a. The endpoint SHALL support boot-time measurement.

   b. The endpoint SHALL use an RTM or a component in the chain of trust for measurement rooted in an RTM to generate BIOS integrity measurements.

   c. The endpoint SHALL use approved standard cryptographic techniques to generate BIOS integrity measurements.

   d. The endpoint SHALL use standard BIOS integrity measurements formats.

   e. The format and reporting of BIMs – both golden measurements and endpoint measurements – SHALL use open standards or specifications, such as [TCG-Manifest] and [TCG-Integrity].

   f. The endpoint vendor SHOULD use an extensible system to enable adding support for measuring option ROMs, etc.

   g. The endpoint SHALL store BIMs in an RTS.

   h. The endpoint vendor SHOULD make raw BIOS configuration data available for reporting and SHOULD have a means of interpretation of that data available.

3. Measurement Log

   a. BIOS functions SHALL record in an SML measurement and event extensions into the CIMR and DIMR.

   b. BIOS functions SHOULD record in an SML measurement and event extensions into the PIMR.

   c. BIOS functions SHALL use a standardized format, such as [TCG-ConvBiosSpec], when recording BIM and other BIOS-related events in an SML.

   d. BIOS SHALL ensure the proper handoff of the SML to the post-boot environment.

4. Measurement Support

   a. The OS vendor SHALL support a standard API for collecting measurements.

   b. The endpoint, OS, and application vendors SHALL support an RTR for collecting and reporting BIMs.

Section 3.3.2, Security Guidelines for the Reporting Protocol

1. BIOS reporting mechanisms MAY prepare and issue a BIOS integrity report to an authenticated MAA upon any of the following conditions:

   a. When a change was made to the BIOS configuration

   b. When a change was made to the BIOS software

   c. When a local port was used to access the BIOS or its configuration

   d. When a BIOS error condition has been generated

   e. Upon connection to a network controlled by an authenticated MAA.

2. BIOS reporting mechanisms MAY support the ability to configure specific events to trigger reports of BIOS integrity measurements.

3. Report requests MAY be initiated by either the reporter or the receiver of the report. The following requirements apply to requests that are initiated by either side:

   a. Mechanisms SHALL be capable of providing provably fresh BIOS reports that are sent to the MAA.

b. The report SHOULD include a reference to the formatting standard/schema used for the report.

c. The report format SHOULD include a version field that can be updated over time as the report format gets extended or otherwise changes.

d. All requests to issue or provide a report from an unauthenticated entity SHOULD be ignored.

e. Requests to provide or issue a report MAY contain a priority that indicates the urgency of the request.

f. Response timeframes related to requests MAY be configurable by the licensed user based on priority.

Section 3.4.2, Security Guidelines for Measurement Collection and Transmission

The Transmission Agent SHALL securely transmit measurements of BIOS integrity from endpoints to the MAA, as follows:

1. All reporting sessions SHALL:

    a. have the ability to provide confidentiality protection.

    b. provide integrity protection and freshness.

    c. authenticate the MAA.

    d. provide authentication of endpoint identities.

2. The Transmission Agent:

    a. SHALL permit measurements to be integrity protected all the way from the RTR to the verifying component.

    b. SHOULD support a variety of different services such as continuous monitoring, network access control, and application-layer integrity monitoring

    c. SHOULD ensure the resulting system is inexpensive, unobtrusive, high performance, and secure (although higher levels of security may require higher levels of cost)

3. Collection Agents and Transmission Agents on endpoints SHOULD support open standards that enable interoperability among many different kinds of endpoints and MAAs over many different forms of communications media, to the extent that such standards are available.

Section 3.5.2, Security Guidelines for the MAA

1. The MAA SHALL be capable of storing expected values (golden measurements).

2. The MAA SHALL be capable of comparing new reported values against expected values and/or previously reported (last known) measurements

3. The MAA SHALL be capable of storing reported values.

4. MAAs SHALL support open standards that enable interoperability among many different kinds of endpoints and MAAs over many different forms of communications media, to the extent that such standards are available.

5. The MAA MAY be capable of providing an assessment of the likelihood that an unexpected, anomalous measurement is the result of a bit rot, if provided with the contents of the BIOS that generated the anomalous measurement as well as the BIOS contents for which golden measurements exist.

Appendix B—Glossary and Abbreviations

This portion of the appendix defines terms used in this document.

Attribute: A property of RoTs used by an assessor to determine how much trust to place in them.

BIOS Code Integrity Measurement Register (CIMR): A register that contains either the cryptographic hash of all the static BIOS code on the endpoint or a composite of hashes of all the BIOS components that make up the BIOS code space.

BIOS Data Integrity Measurement Register (DIMR): A register that contains either the cryptographic hash of all the dynamic BIOS configuration data on the endpoint or a composite of hashes of all the BIOS components that make up the BIOS configuration data space.

BIOS Privacy Integrity Measurement Register (PIMR): A register that contains a composite of hashes of all BIOS privacy sensitive data.

BIOS integrity measurement generation: The act of creating hashes of BIOS components and filling static and dynamic BIOS configuration registers with those hashes.

Bit rot: Modifications to BIOS storage caused by random physical processes.

Collection: Both the act of measuring the BIOS integrity of an endpoint and the process of gathering the resulting measurements so that they can be transmitted from the endpoint.

Dynamic BIOS Components: Those portions of the BIOS which the user may change without assistance from either the BIOS vendor or the system vendor. This is often referred to as BIOS configuration data.

Endpoint: A system whose BIOS integrity is being measured. An endpoint can be a laptop, a server, a virtualized environment, a service, etc.

Golden measurements: A trusted set of integrity measurements for a BIOS and its configuration data. These measurements are usually provided from a trusted party, such as the OEM of the endpoint, or they are taken by system administrators during the initial provisioning of a device. The SHA-2 hash of BIOS signed by an OEM would be an example of a golden BIOS measurement. A golden BIOS measurement does not confer information regarding the presence or absence of malicious properties. It does aid in the quick, authentic, non-reputable identification of an object.

Integrity measurement: A compact representation of a binary code and/or data. In the context of BIOS integrity measurement, this is typically represented as a cryptographic hash of binary code and data, often cryptographically signed to preserve authenticity and non-repudiation.

Known-good state: When the BIOS has been verified as being in an acceptable state. An example of this state is when a digital signature of the loaded BIOS verifies as matching the manufacturer's current version.

Measurement Assessment Authority (MAA): An agent running on behalf of IT management which receives measurements from clients, checks the signature of those measurements, assesses the quality of the measurements by comparing them with golden measurements, may further analyze measurements (to determine what changes have been made to BIOS integrity measurements if the measurements do not match golden measurements), and then either displays the results to IT management or acts as a proxy for IT management to automatically take preset action when the measurements are not expected values.

Management controller: In a server environment, there is often a supervisory processor or controller that "manages" the primary processors running applications. This management controller is separate from the primary processors and can perform various operations on them or on their behalf.

Primary processor: One of possibly several processors (cores) that is available to run applications on a system.

Remediation: The process of correcting a problem with a computing system.

Root of Trust (RoT): A component (software, hardware, or hybrid) and a computing engine that constitute a set of unconditionally trusted functions. An RoT must always behave in an expected manner because its misbehavior cannot be detected.

Root of Trust for Measurement (RTM): A computing engine capable of making inherently reliable integrity measurements. The RTM is the root of the chain of transitive trust for subsequent measurement agents.

Root of Trust for Reporting (RTR): A computing engine capable of reliably reporting information provided by the RTM and its measurement agent(s) or held by the RTS.

Root of Trust for Storage (RTS): A computing engine capable of maintaining a tamper-evident summary of integrity measurement values and the sequence of those measurements.

Static BIOS components – Those portions of the BIOS which the user may change, usually with assistance either from the BIOS vendor or the system vendor. This is often referred to as BIOS code. Historically, this code contained few protections against change. [NIST-SP800-147] outlines BIOS protections that vendors could deploy.

The following list contains the acronyms and other abbreviations used in this document.

ACPI (Advanced Configuration and Power Interface)

API (Application Programming Interface)

ARF (Asset Reporting Format)

BBM (BIOS-Based Management)

BIM (BIOS Integrity Measurement)

BIOS (Basic Input/Output System)

CIM (Common Information Model)

CIMR (Code Integrity Measurement Register)

CPU (Central Processing Unit)

DIM (Desktop Management Interface)

DIMR (Data Integrity Measurement Register)

DMTF (Distributed Management Task Force)

EFI (Extensible Firmware Interface)

FIPS (Federal Information Processing Standard)

HMAC (Hash-Based Message Authentication Code)

IMR (Integrity Measurement Register)

ISV (Independent Software Vendor)

IT (Information Technology)

ITL (Information Technology Laboratory)

MAA (Measurement Assessment Authority)

NFC (Near Field Communication)

NIST (National Institute of Standards and Technology)

NISTIR (National Institute of Standards and Technology Interagency Report)

OEM (Original Equipment Manufacturer)

OS (Operating System)

PCR (Endpoint Configuration Register)

PIMR (Privacy Integrity Measurement Register)

POST (Power On Self Test)

PXE (Preboot Execution Environment)

RAM (Random Access Memory)

RFC (Request for Comment)

ROM (Read Only Memory)

RoT (Root of Trust)

RTM (Root of Trust for Measurement)

RTR (Root of Trust for Reporting)

RTS (Root of Trust for Storage)

SCAP (Security Content Automation Protocol)

SMBIOS (System Management Basic Input/Output System)

SML (Stored Measurement Log)

SMM (System Management Mode)

SMRAM (System Management Random Access Memory)

SP (Special Publication)

TCG (Trusted Computing Group)

TLS (Transport Layer Security)

TLV (Type-length-value)

TNC (Trusted Network Connect)

TPM (Trusted Platform Module)

UEFI (Unified Extensible Firmware Interface)

URI (Uniform Resource Identifier)

USB (Universal Serial Bus)

VAR (Value Added Reseller)

VM (Virtual Machine)

XML (Extensible Markup Language)

Appendix C—References

Appendix C identifies relevant references.

[DMTF-SMBIOS] DSP0134, "System Management BIOS (SMBIOS) Reference Specification", Version 2.7.1, DMTF, February 2011, http://www.dmtf.org/standards/smbios.

[IETF-RFC-2119] Bradner, S., RFC 2119, "Key words for use in RFCs to Indicate Requirement Levels", IETF, March 1997, http://www.ietf.org/rfc/rfc2119.txt.

[IETF-RFC-3576] Chiba, M., Dommety, G., Eklund, M., Mitton, D., and Aboba, B., RFC 3576, "Dynamic Authorization Extensions to Remote Authentication Dial In User Service (RADIUS)", IETF, July 2003, http://www.ietf.org/rfc/rfc3576.txt.

[IETF-RFC-5792] Sangster, P. and Narayan, K., RFC 5792, "PA-TNC: A Posture Attribute (PA) Protocol Compatible with Trusted Network Connect (TNC)", IETF, March 2010, http://www.ietf.org/rfc/rfc5792.txt.

[IETF-RFC-5793] Sahita, R., Hanna, S., Hurst, R., and Narayan, K., RFC 5793, "PB-TNC: A Posture Broker (PB) Protocol Compatible with Trusted Network Connect (TNC)", IETF, March 2010, http://www.ietf.org/rfc/rfc5793.txt.

[NIST-FIPS180-3] FIPS PUB 180-3, "Secure Hash Standard (SHS)", NIST, October 2008, http://csrc.nist.gov/publications/fips/fips180-3/fips180-3_final.pdf.

[NIST-IR-7670] Waltermire, D., Johnson, C., Kerr, M., Wojcik, M., and Wunder, J., IR 7670 (Draft), "Proposed Open Specifications for an Enterprise Remediation Automation Framework", NIST, February 2011, http://csrc.nist.gov/publications/drafts/nistir-7670/Draft-NISTIR-7670_Feb2011.pdf.

[NIST-IR-7694] Halbardier, A., Waltermire, D., and Johnson, M., IR 7694, "Specification for the Asset Reporting Format 1.1 (ARF)", NIST, June 2011, http://csrc.nist.gov/publications/PubsNISTIRs.html#NIST-IR-7694.

[NIST-IR-7802] Booth, H. and Halbardier, A., IR 7802, "Trust Model for Security Automation Data 1.0 (TMSAD)", NIST, September 2011, http://csrc.nist.gov/publications/PubsNISTIRs.html#NIST-IR-7802.

[NIST-SP800-106] Dang, Q., SP 800-106, "Randomized Hashing for Digital Signatures", NIST, February 2009, http://csrc.nist.gov/publications/PubsSPs.html#800-106.

[NIST-SP800-126] Waltermire, D., Quinn, S., Scarfone, K., and Halbardier, A., SP 800-126 Revision 2, "The Technical Specification for Security Content Automation Protocol (SCAP): SCAP Version 1.2", NIST, September 2011, http://csrc.nist.gov/publications/PubsSPs.html#800-126.

[NIST-SP800-147] Cooper, D., Polk, W., Regenscheid, A., and Souppaya, M., "NIST Special Publication 800-147: BIOS Protection Guidelines", NIST, April 2011, http://csrc.nist.gov/publications/PubsSPs.html#800-147.

[TCG-ARCH-INTER] "TCG Trusted Network Connect TNC Architecture for Interoperability", Version 1.4, Revision 4, Trusted Computing Group, May 2009, http://www.trustedcomputinggroup.org/resources/tnc_architecture_for_interoperability_specification.

[TCG-Att-PTS] "TCG Attestation PTS Protocol: Binding to TNC IF-M", Version 1.0, Revision 28, Trusted Computing Group, August 2011, http://www.trustedcomputinggroup.org/resources/tcg_attestation_pts_protocol_binding_to_tnc_ifm.

[TCG-ConvBiosSpec] "TCG PC Client Specific Implementation Specification for Conventional BIOS", Version 1.20, Trusted Computing Group, July 2005, http://www.trustedcomputinggroup.org/resources/pc_client_work_group_specific_implementation_specification_for_conventional_bios_specification_version_12.

[TCG-EFI] "TCG EFI Platform Specification", Version 1.20, Revision 1.0, June 2006, http://www.trustedcomputinggroup.org/resources/tcg_efi_platform_specification_version_120_revision_10.

[TCG-IF-M] "TCG Trusted Network Connect TNC IF-M: TLV Binding", Version 1.0, Revision 37, Trusted Computing Group, March 2010, http://www.trustedcomputinggroup.org/resources/tnc_ifm_tlv_binding_specification.

[TCG-IF-PEP] "TCG Trusted Network Connect TNC IF-PEP: Protocol Bindings for RADIUS", Version 1.1, Revision 0.7, Trusted Computing Group, February 2007, http://www.trustedcomputinggroup.org/resources/tnc_ifpep_protocol_bindings_for_radius_specification.

[TCG-IF-PTS] "TCG Infrastructure Working Group Platform Trust Services Interface Specification (IF-PTS)", Version 1.0, Revision 1.0, November 2006, http://www.trustedcomputinggroup.org/resources/infrastructure_work_group_platform_trust_services_interface_specification_version_10.

[TCG-IF-T-EAP] "TCG Trusted Network Connect TNC IF-T: Protocol Bindings for Tunneled EAP Methods", Version 1.1, Revision 10, Trusted Computing Group, May 2007, http://www.trustedcomputinggroup.org/resources/tnc_ift_protocol_bindings_for_tunneled_eap_methods_specification.

[TCG-IF-T-TLS] "TCG Trusted Network Connect TNC IF-T: Binding to TLS", Version 1.0, Revision 16, Trusted Computing Group, May 2009, http://www.trustedcomputinggroup.org/resources/tnc_ift_binding_to_tls_version_10_revision_16.

[TCG-Integrity] "TCG Infrastructure Working Group Integrity Report Schema Specification", Version 1.0, Trusted Computing Group, November 2006, http://www.trustedcomputinggroup.org/resources/infrastructure_work_group_integrity_report_schema_specification_version_10/.

[TCG-Manifest] "TCG Infrastructure Working Group Reference Manifest (RM) Schema Specification", Version 1.0, Trusted Computing Group, November 2006, http://www.trustedcomputinggroup.org/resources/infrastructure_work_group_reference_manifest_rm_schema_specification_version_10/.

Appendix D—Options for Implementing Roots of Trust

The basis of BIOS integrity guarantees are RoTs that are founded on the properties of one or more hardware mechanisms. Some of these RoT themselves assume that the requirements and recommendations in [NIST-SP800-147] are met. Some of the most relevant hardware mechanisms for RoTs are enumerated below. (This list is not comprehensive.)

D.1   Startup Logic of the CPU and Chipset

BIOS integrity depends on the behavior of the CPU being well defined at startup, and in particular on the chipset correctly mapping the BIOS storage device and the CPU executing the correct initial BIOS instruction, as expected, after a reset. This hardware mechanism is the basis for boot-time RTMs, but may be less relevant for RTMs based on "late-launch" mechanisms or runtime re-initialization of the CPU.

D.2   UEFI Power-On SEC Security Phase

The Unified Extensible Firmware Interface (UEFI) provides a supplement and partial replacement for functions previously entirely handled by BIOS. The UEFI Power-on SEC security phase may provide an RoT that may be able to reliably invoke software measurement agents in the UEFI in a way that can be used to implement an RTM for BIOS integrity. This may require compliance with [NIST-SP800-147].

D.3   Access-Controlled Regions of the BIOS Storage Device

The integrity of the BIOS and of BIOS measurements may be based on hardware access control mechanisms for the BIOS storage device itself. Such access control can be enforced through set-until-reboot latches that prevent reads or writes to the BIOS storage device. Such latches remain set until the next hardware reset and can be locked down, for example, by the BIOS itself, during early stages of the boot. The latches may be implemented, for example, through hardware mechanisms in either the BIOS storage device itself or in the CPU chipset. These mechanisms may be used to form the basis of compliance with [NIST-SP800-147].

Access-controlled regions of the BIOS storage device supported by [NIST-SP800-147] compliant architectures can also serve as a basis for RTSs or RTRs. For example, the BIOS may measure itself during initialization and place the measurement results in a readable, but write-protected-until-hardware-reset BIOS storage region. The BIOS can also create reports using a cryptographic key stored within a region of the BIOS storage that is subsequently rendered inaccessible until the next hardware reset, before the BIOS passes control to the OS or boot loader. To guarantee freshness, reports can make use of nonces stored in volatile areas of the BIOS during the previous OS execution.

D.3.1   Static Immutable BIOS Boot Block

A static immutable BIOS Boot Block (or Initial BIOS code region) can serve a basis for BIOS integrity RTMs, e.g., by measuring the contents of the relevant BIOS storage device and by setting its access-control latches. By being built on an immutable BIOS boot block, such an RTM could possibly provide Mutable State Tolerance, as defined in Section 3.1 even without complying with [NIST-SP800-147].

D.4   Isolated CPU Execution Modes and Access-Controlled Memory

Several CPU execution modes and memory access-control features may form RoTs for BIOS integrity and for BIOS measurements. By their nature, these implementations cannot provide Memory Disclosure Tolerance, as defined in Section 3.1.

With a [NIST-SP800-147] architecture, the SMM execution mode of the CPU is a potential RoT that can be the basis for isolated, stateful mechanisms that are controlled and initialized by the BIOS at boot time, but are available during the machine's entire execution, until the next reboot. In some cases, SMM code can have greater access to the BIOS storage device than the OS kernel. SMM mode on its own is not a basis for RTMs. However, SMM mode can build on a BIOS-based RTM and serve to (a) perform runtime measurements of the contents and the relevant access-control latch settings of the BIOS storage device, (b) implement an RTS by placing measurement results in SMRAM, or (c) implement an RTR, for example by having the BIOS initialize SMRAM with a private cryptographic key, used to sign measurement reports, and which is accessible nowhere else but from SMM mode after BIOS initialization has finished.

As outlined in the TCG specifications, some CPUs provide support for so-called dynamic RoTs, where the CPU is reinitialized into a known-good state. In combination with a TPM, such "late-launch" CPU execution modes can be the basis for all necessary RoTs. However, notably, such dynamic measurement may not be able to establish the integrity of the BIOS or BIOS settings at past or future hardware resets; to establish such boot-time guarantees, BIOS integrity MUST be protected using mechanisms such as outlined in [NIST-SP800-147].

D.5   Supervisor CPU Execution Modes and Supervisor-Only Memory

A traditional role of privileged, kernel-mode code in hypervisors or operating systems is protection of system devices, such as the BIOS. A hypervisor or an OS kernel is nearly always protected through hardware-supported memory mechanisms, and the kernel runs in a supervisor execution mode with its own private memory. In principle, those hardware mechanisms can be the RoT for implementing BIOS integrity RTMs, RTSs, and RTRs, with the hypervisor or OS protecting its own integrity, that of the BIOS, and that of reported measurements, particularly assuming a [NIST-SP800-147] architecture. Due to their size and complexity, such hypervisor or OS-supported RoTs are likely to provide few guarantees, and minimal assurance, at least for standard hypervisors or OSs.

D.6   Trusted Platform Modules

TPMs can serve as a basis for RTSs and RTRs. When combined with static immutable BIOS boot blocks (as dictated by the TCG specifications, and as in Section D.3), TPMs can provide for both Mutable State Tolerance and Memory Disclosure Tolerance, as defined in Section 3.1.

D.7   Proprietary RoTs

BIOS integrity protection and measurement mechanisms can be implemented by custom logic in the CPU, CPU chipsets, and/or the BIOS storage device. Such custom logic may be used to implement any RoTs, although few (if any) such implementations are currently available for commodity client hardware platforms.

Examples of such RoTs might include BIOS storage devices that are either packaged with or closely communicate with an embedded, separate microcontroller that is provisioned with a private key and private storage. If properly implemented, such an RoT can be used to implement mechanisms that provide Mutable State Tolerance and Memory Disclosure Tolerance, as defined in Section 3.1.

Appendix E—Example Implementation Possibilities

Appendix E enumerates some possibilities for the implementation of BIOS integrity measurements, using commonly available mechanisms. Some examples of mechanisms not considered here are management controllers (e.g., as the embedded management engine in Intel's Sandy Bridge and successor chipsets), as well as microcontrollers embedded into BIOS storage devices.

E.1   Example 1 - Possible implementation using a high-assurance kernel or hypervisor

In this example implementation, a trusted supervisor (such as a trustworthy hypervisor or high-assurance separation kernel) is used to create the necessary RoTs for BIOS integrity measurements, based on the CPU startup logic (Section E.1) and supervisor execution modes (Section E.4, item 3) hardware RoTs. The supervisor is responsible for inductively protecting the RoTs as well as ensuring the integrity of the BIOS and its settings during operation and across updates.

1. At a machine reset, the CPU starts executing the first instruction of the BIOS out of the BIOS storage device (e.g., flash chip).

2. The BIOS completes initialization and turns control directly over to a trusted supervisor, or to a trusted bootloader which finds and loads the trusted supervisor.

3. The trusted supervisor is responsible for implementing the [NIST-SP800-147] guidelines and for completely mediating and controlling access to the machine configuration, including the configuration of the CPU startup logic and the BIOS contents and settings, as well as the configuration of the boot storage device containing the bootloader and the code and configuration of the supervisor itself.

4. The trusted supervisor also forms the RTM, RTS, and RTR for BIOS integrity measurements, and must protect stored measurement results (e.g., as part of the protected state on the boot storage device) and allow those results to be provably freshly reported (e.g., so they cannot be spoofed or replayed). For this purpose, the supervisor may make use of secret or private keys, for example stored in the BIOS or boot storage devices.

5. Whether on demand, on boot, or at time of BIOS upgrade, the supervisor can prepare BIM reports by measuring such things as (a) all BIOS code and (b) all critical BIOS data, such as non-writable configuration settings, and (c) the NVRAM configuration data.

6. It is the responsibility of the BIOS and the supervisor to ensure that the supervisor (and only the supervisor) will again be booted after the next hardware reset. The BIOS must protect itself and any stored RTR cryptographic keys (e.g., by destroying those keys), unless the BIOS can establish that control will pass to a verified copy of the trusted supervisor after BIOS initialization finishes.

The above implementation provides neither the Mutable State Tolerance nor Memory Disclosure Tolerance properties described in Section 3.1.

E.2   Example 2 - Possible implementation using latch-based mechanisms

In this example implementation, which assumes a [NIST-SP800-147] architecture, a combination of BIOS startup code and SMM code installed by the BIOS at startup is used to create the necessary RoTs for BIOS integrity measurements, based on the CPU startup logic (Section D.1), SMM execution mode (Section D.4), and BIOS storage device access control (Section D.3) hardware RoTs. The BIOS itself and its SMM code is responsible for inductively protecting the RoTs as well as ensuring the integrity of the BIOS and its settings during operation and across updates.

1. At a machine reset, the CPU starts executing the first instruction of the BIOS out of the BIOS storage device (e.g., flash chip).

2. To implement the [NIST-SP800-147] guidelines the BIOS first checks if a valid, signed BIOS upgrade is available in accessible storage (e.g., on disk, in free space in the BIOS flash chip, or in an inserted USB key). Finding no upgrade is needed, the BIOS may check its own integrity; this should only be needed to guard against bit rot, since BIOS integrity is inductively preserved through runtime write-protection.

3. The BIOS then sets up SMM mode and copies a BIOS-specific private key into SMRAM. The BIOS also makes a copy of all its BIOS/NVRAM configuration data to SMRAM. SMM code is responsible for runtime BIOS measurements and the key signs BIM results.

4. The BIOS then programs locked-until-machine-reset latches to (a) make non-writable all BIOS code and all critical data, such as non-writable configuration settings, and (b) make inaccessible, i.e., non-readable and non-writable, the BIOS flash region containing the BIOS-specific private key.

5. The BIOS turns control over to the bootloader, which finds and loads an OS.

6. At runtime, a nonce is provided to create a report on a BIM attribute, such as, for instance, (a) the BIOS code bytes in the BIOS flash chip, (b) the current or boot-time NVRAM configuration, (c) the state of the locked-until-machine-reset latches and related machine control areas, etc.

7. SMM code is invoked, via one or more SMIs, and the SMM code measures the asked for attribute, such as, for (c) by querying the control registers in the BIOS flash chip itself and in the chipset (e.g., the southbridge).

8. The SMM code combines its measurements with the nonce into a message digest, and signs that digest with the BIOS-specific private key.

The above implementation provides neither the Mutable State Tolerance nor Memory Disclosure Tolerance properties described in Section 3.1.

E.3   Example 3 - Possible implementation using TPM-based mechanisms

In this example implementation, common in enterprise clients today, a combination of BIOS startup code and the TCG-specified TPM is used to create the necessary RoTs for BIOS integrity measurements, based on the CPU startup logic (Section D.1), TPM (Section D.5), and BIOS storage-device access control (Section D.3) hardware RoTs. The BIOS itself is responsible for inductively protecting the Software Measurement Agents as well as ensuring the integrity of the BIOS and its settings during operation and across updates.

1. At a machine reset, the CPU starts executing the first instruction of an immutable BIOS boot block out of the BIOS storage device, and the TPM registers are set to known values.

2. The immutable BIOS boot block measures (a) all BIOS code and (b) all critical BIOS data, such as non-writable configuration settings, and (c) the NVRAM configuration data and extends these measurements into separate PCRs on the TPM. The TPM is responsible for storing measurements and reporting BIM results, and the TPM key is used to sign BIM results.

3. The BIOS boot block turns control over to code resident in the measured, mutable parts of the BIOS storage device, which in turn passes control to the bootloader to find and load an OS. Note

that this implementation does NOT meet [NIST-SP800-147], since no attempt is made to establish BIOS code integrity, e.g., by write-protecting code regions in the BIOS storage device.

4. At runtime, a nonce is provided to create a report on a BIM attribute, such as, for instance, (a) the BIOS code hash, (b) the boot-time NVRAM configuration, (c) the state of the locked-until-machine-reset latches and related machine control areas, etc.

5. A PCR register in the TPM is combined with the nonce, and signed by the TPM-resident key, to create a report on, for example, the BIOS code and configuration present at boot time.

E.4   Example 4 - Possible implementation using CPU-late-launch-based mechanisms

In this example implementation, a combination of BIOS startup code and the TCG-compliant CPU late-launch is used to create the necessary RoTs for BIOS integrity measurements, based on the CPU startup logic (Section D.1), TPM (Section D.5), and runtime re-initialized CPU execution mode (Section D.4) hardware RoTs. The hardware itself is responsible for inductively protecting the RoTs, while the integrity of the BIOS and its settings during operation and across updates may be protected via various software means—or even not protected at all.

1. At a machine reset, the CPU starts executing the first instruction of the BIOS out of the BIOS storage device.

2. A flaw in the implementation of [NIST-SP800-147] guidelines may have allowed the BIOS to be corrupted. However, the late-launch facilities allow BIOS integrity to be measured in a way that will reveal this corruption, potentially revealing an attack.

3. The BIOS turns control over to the bootloader, which finds and loads an OS.

4. At runtime, a nonce is provided to create a report on a BIM attribute, such as, for instance, (a) the BIOS code hash, (b) the NVRAM configuration, (c) the state of the locked-until-machine-reset latches and related machine control areas, etc.

5. The CPU enters a clean, well-defined environment through late-launch facilities, with known, well-defined values in some TPM registers.

6. The late-launch environment measures such things as (a) all BIOS code and (b) all critical BIOS data, such as non-writable configuration settings, and (c) the NVRAM configuration data and writes to well-defined, separate PCRs on the TPM. The TPM is responsible for storing measurements and reporting BIM results, and the TPM key is used to sign BIM results.

7. A PCR register in the TPM is combined with the nonce, and signed by the TPM-resident key, to create a report on, for example, the BIOS code present at boot time.

www.ingramcontent.com/pod-product-compliance
Lightning Source LLC
Chambersburg PA
CBHW060459060326
40689CB00020B/4591